The Couple and Family in Managed Care

Assessment, Evaluation, and Treatment

Mental Health Practice Under Managed Care
A Brunner/Mazel Book Series

S. Richard Sauber, Ph.D., Series Editor

The Brunner/Mazel Mental Health Practice Under Managed Care Series addresses the major developments and changes resulting from the introduction of managed care. Volumes in the series will enable mental health professionals to provide effective therapy to their patients while conducting and maintaining a successful practice.

4. The Couple and Family in Managed Care: Assessment, Evaluation, and Treatment
   By Dennis A. Bagarozzi, Ph.D.

3. Solution-Oriented Brief Therapy for Adjustment Disorders: A Guide for Providers Under Managed Care
   By Daniel L. Araoz, Ed.D., and Marie A. Carrese, Ph.D.

2. Group Psychotherapy and Managed Mental Health Care: A Clinical Guide for Providers
   By Henry I. Spitz, M.D.

1. Psychopharmacology and Psychotherapy: Strategies for Maximizing Treatment Outcomes
   By Len Sperry, M.D., Ph.D.

Mental Health Practice Under Managed Care, Volume 4

The Couple and Family in Managed Care

Assessment, Evaluation, and Treatment

Dennis A. Bagarozzi, Ph.D.

Brunner/Mazel, *Publishers* ● New York

Library of Congress Cataloging-in-Publication Data

Bagarozzi, Dennis A.
 The couple and family in managed care : assessment, evaluation, and treatment / Dennis A. Bagarozzi.
  p. cm. – (Mental health practice under managed care ; v. 4.)
 Includes bibliographical references (p.) and index.
 ISBN 0-87630-810-8 (pbk.)
 1. Family psychotherapy. 2. Marital psychotherapy. 3. Managed mental health care. 4. Family assessment. I. Title. II. Series.
RC488.5.B269   1996
616.89'156–dc20   96-16041
                                                              CIP

Published by
BRUNNER/MAZEL, INC.
19 Union Square West
New York, New York 10003

Manufactured in the United States of America

10   9   8   7   6   5   4   3   2   1

Contents

INTRODUCTION   vii

1. Pretreatment Assessment and Decision
   Making: The Initial Interview   1

2. Individual Diagnoses and Marital/Family
   Assessment: A Complementary Process   11

3. Choosing Appropriate Assessment Instruments
   for Marital and Family Intervention   22

4. The Assessment Interview: The Case of
   Mr. and Mrs. M.   51

5. Assessment in Crisis Situations: The Case of
   Ron and Sara   72

6. Assessment of Developmental Transitions:
   The Case of Mr. and Mrs. Z.   84

7. Assessments in Context: Two Case Studies–
   Nuclear Family and Intergenerational Systems   93

8. Accountability in Managed Mental Health
   Care Practice   118

REFERENCES   147

NAME INDEX   155

SUBJECT INDEX   159

Introduction

At the present time, most managed mental health care organizations do not extend their coverage to include V-Code conditions listed in the DSM-IV as a routine part of their benefit packages. Conditions that fall within the V-Code include marital problems, family problems, adolescent developmental problems, normal bereavements and grief reactions, life stage transitional problems, and other life stage circumstantial difficulties. Under some managed mental health care contracts, V-Code conditions may be handled separately through Employee Assistance Program (EAP) provisions.

There are some managed mental health care organizations, however, that will allow (for a limited number of sessions) a therapist to treat the identified patient's spouse and/or other family members under certain conditions. These collateral contacts, as they are called, may also be approved for the treatment of some interpersonal sexual problems that cannot be treated adequately without the full participation of one's spouse. In all cases where collateral contacts are deemed appropriate, prior approval usually must be received from a managed mental health care administrator, such as a case manager, senior clinician, or review specialist.

It is very important to understand that collateral contacts are always seen as adjuncts to individual treatments. In managed mental health care practice, the focus is the individual and the resolution of the problem that brought him/her in for therapy. Involving a spouse or other family members in the treatment does not mean that the focus of treatment changes; that is, including one's spouse and/or one's children does not mean that the primary focus of therapy shifts from the client beneficiary to the treatment of the marital or family system. It simply means that the clinician judges (and the managed mental health care administrator agrees) that the client beneficiary's presenting problem can be treated *more quickly and more successfully* if certain key individuals are actively engaged in the therapeutic process.

When collateral involvements are judged to be necessary, marital and family evaluations (L'Abate & Bagarozzi, 1992) should be used in addition to any individually focused assessment tools or diagnostic procedures. How these instruments are selected and employed in managed mental health care practice is the subject of this volume.

It is important for the reader to understand, as he/she reads through this text, that its major emphasis is not on the *treatment* of marital and family systems, but on *assessment* within the context and confines of managed mental health care practice. In a previous publication (Bagarozzi & Anderson, 1989), a very elaborate and systematic pretreatment–posttreatment and follow-up procedure for evaluating the outcome of marital and family therapy was described. The treatment approaches discussed in that book were of two types. Each could be applied independently or used in tandem, depending on the nature of the presenting problem.

1. Brief and short-term, problem-focused strategies and intervention procedures that are designed to bring about observable behavioral changes in individuals, marital dyads, and family systems.

2. Long-term, time-unlimited, issue- and process-focused intervention strategies that are meant to bring about fundamental changes in the intrapsychic and cognitive structures of individuals, and symbol-focused interventions crafted to produce gradual changes in the dysfunctional structural arrangements of distressed marriages and family systems.

The former treatment approach is the one most compatible with managed mental health care philosophies. Therefore, all treatment examples used in this book are based on brief and short-term, problem-focused work with couples and family systems.

In the first chapter, a specific outline for conducting an initial, behaviorally focused interview designed to pinpoint the presenting problem and to assess whether collateral contacts are necessary is presented for the reader.

In the second chapter, the complementary processes of individual diagnosis and systems-focused evaluation are discussed. Issues having to do with instrument construction, reliability, validity, and clinical utility are briefly reviewed, and a very simple model for making situational-contextual assessments is presented.

Chapter 3 is devoted to the selection of marital and family assessment instruments and describes how instruments are used to refine and expedite the therapeutic process. This process is contrasted with more formal and lengthy evaluation procedures. Modified versions of relationship histories, observational procedures for evaluating couples' communication styles and patterns, and couples' problem-identification guidelines and incentive analyses developed for use in managed mental health care practice are also presented. In addition, a brief measure of marital satisfaction that can be used as an outcome measure in managed mental health care work is described. The Pragmatic Marital Assessment Questionnaire, also developed exclusively for managed mental health care work, is offered for review.

Chapter 4 is devoted to some detailed case interviews that demonstrate the complementary processes of individual assessment and marital evaluation.

In Chapter 5, an additional case of marital treatment is presented, one that highlights a couple in crisis. How assessments are done when couples present with a crisis is demonstrated. The importance of the structuring of the session, the therapist's activity, and the use of *partialization* to help the couple focus on immediate concrete issues that lend themselves to behavioral solutions are presented as well. The clinical interviewing techniques described in the case example bring to the fore the types of therapeutic strategies that can be used to help couples gain the most from treatment in the short time allotted for collateral work under most current managed mental health care arrangements.

Chapter 6 offers, through case material, a clear view of the clinical refinement process. How one goes about selecting assessment aids that are best suited for helping couples quickly identify specific intersystemic issues that are causing them difficulty is demonstrated. This rounds out the discussion of couple assessment procedures.

Issues of therapist/systems fit and compatibility are addressed in Chapter 7, and salient issues related to this very important topic are outlined. Nuclear family and intergenerational assessments are also considered in this chapter.

The final chapter is devoted to issues of accountability in managed mental health care practice. Suggestions for conducting outcome research are offered and different viewpoints concerning clinical evaluation and effectiveness are presented to the reader as food for thought.

The Couple and Family in Managed Care

Assessment, Evaluation, and Treatment

1

Pretreatment Assessment and Decision Making: The Initial Interview

The goals of the initial interview are threefold: (1) to establish a trusting therapeutic relationship with client beneficiaries, (2) to gather as much relevant information about the presenting problem as possible, and (3) to help the client beneficiaries begin to conceptualize their presenting problems in a concrete, behaviorally specific way that makes short-term, behavioral intervention possible.

It is assumed that all therapists who serve on managed mental health care panels possess the skills necessary for establishing and maintaining a meaningful therapeutic relationship with client beneficiaries; therefore, the requisite skills for doing so will only be listed and not reviewed in any detail. For a comprehensive discussion of the skills listed below, the reader is referred to Bagarozzi (1983a). These skills include attending; accurate empathic understanding; unconditional positive regard; respect; nonpossessive warmth; genuineness; congruence of self and congruence of communication; self-involvement; appropriate self-disclosure; reciprocity; exchange; relational accommodation; role taking; perspective reversal and decentering; immediacy; interpretation; confrontation; information giving; teaching; and the ability to formulate directives and give homework assignments.

The questions presented on pages 5–7 can be used to help the therapist gather relevant information about the nature and scope of

1

the presenting problem. They not only help the therapist determine if and when collateral contacts are warranted, but also help the client beneficiary begin to see and conceptualize his/her difficulties in ways that make concrete and behavioral solutions more likely. An important aspect of the initial interview is the empowerment of the client beneficiary. The therapist is responsible for creating an atmosphere in which mutual collaboration is the order of business. From the outset, he/she must make it clear that the client beneficiary is expected to become an active participant in a problem-solving process. For many client beneficiaries, active involvement and participation in resolving the difficulties that bring them in for therapy is something for which they have not been prepared. Frequently, they think of themselves as "sick patients" who will play a passive role vis-à-vis a "doctor" or some other "mental health" professional. Changing their conception of themselves and their role in therapy is a cognitive reorientation that the therapist must facilitate during the initial interview/fact-finding process. A major thrust of therapy during this initial stage is to enhance the client beneficiary's sense of personal efficacy and mastery.

The therapist's first responsibility is to help the client beneficiaries describe their presenting problem in behaviorally specific terms that make it possible to select and apply effective intervention procedures. Many clients may not be accustomed to describing their difficulties in behaviorally specific language. Their descriptions, for the most part, will tend to be global and vague: "I don't have any desire to go to work anymore," "I am having difficulties with my wife/husband," "I don't get along with my boss very well."

It is important for the therapist to understand fully and appreciate the relationship among accurate behavioral problem specification, the selection of appropriate assessment instruments and procedures, and treatment planning. Throughout this process, the therapist must always keep in mind the four cardinal foci of intervention—the client beneficiary's (1) behaviors, (2) affects, (3) cognitions, and (4) the client beneficiary's dysfunctional attitudes about himself/herself that stand in the way of therapeutic progress, successful problem solving, and positive behavior change. Therefore, when inquiring about the nature of the presenting problem, all four domains should be evaluated. For example, if the presenting problem is a client beneficiary's loss of the desire to work, which has resulted in excessive lateness and absence from his job (i.e., the *behavior*) the therapist should help the client explore his feelings (i.e., *affects*) about his job, about himself in relation to his job, and about his superiors, coworkers, and others; *cognitions*—what he thinks and says to himself about his job, his place of employment, his colleagues, superiors, and others, and the contents of his internal dialogues on the days he does not feel like working, as well as on those days when he does go in to work; and his *dysfunctional attitudes* toward work in general and his hopes, aspirations, and expectations for this job in particular. By exploring the client's *affects, attitudes, beliefs,* and *cognitions,* the therapist can begin to get a rounded picture of those factors that contribute to the presenting problem behavior, specifically, loss of the desire to work, frequent lateness, and absenteeism.

An important aspect of helping clients learn how to take an active part in their therapeutic progress is for the therapist to teach them how to conceptualize their presenting problem in a way that increases their personal efficacy and makes active mastery possible. One strategy, *problem codification,* is a technique designed to help the client gain a sense of mastery by reducing the scope and complexity of the presenting problem to discreet behaviors or behavioral sequences that the client can begin to manage. For instance, in the above example, going to work each day and getting to work on time are considered to be codified behavioral descriptions of the presenting problem that have now been reduced to two related, yet discrete, behavioral sequences.

Once this has been done, the client is taught to conceptualize each component of the problem as either a behavioral *deficit* or a behavioral *excess*. In the example cited above, not going to work each day is described as a behavioral deficit while absenteeism is seen as a behavioral excess. The therapeutic goals are to increase the former and decrease the latter.

According to this approach, the therapist is an expert on human behavior who can help the client beneficiary acquire the skills necessary to overcome the presenting problem or problems.

HISTORY OF THE PRESENTING PROBLEM

Within a managed mental health care setting, the therapist must make sure to keep the client beneficiary focused on the presenting problem. Since there are usually a finite number of clinical sessions available to the client beneficiary, it is important to get to the heart of the matter as quickly as possible.

An important determination that the therapist must make in gathering pertinent information about the presenting problem and its history is whether the client beneficiary's problem is one that is *relatively recent* in origin or is a *chronic* one with which the client has been struggling for years. Problems that are of recent origin frequently have their source in the client beneficiary's current life situations and circumstances. On the other hand, *chronic* and *recurrent* problems of long duration may be symptomatic of a more deeply rooted intrapsychic conflict and may represent a dysfunctional thematic style of life (Bagarozzi & Anderson, 1989).

Another important determination that the therapist should make at the outset of treatment is whether the client is seeking treatment *voluntarily* or whether someone, such as an employer, supervisor, or spouse, has recommended professional assistance (as is often the case when employee assistance programs are part of the managed mental health care benefit package). Furthermore, the therapist must ascertain whether the client is truly motivated to correct the problem for which treatment has been recommended.

In either instance—long-standing, chronic, and/or recurring problems and symptoms or mandated treatments—the therapist must appreciate that he/she is dealing with some particularly difficult clinical situations and treatment problems. Since such factors as chronicity and resistance have a direct bearing on the development of a positive therapeutic relationship, the therapist's efficacy, and the overall success of planned intervention, these potential stumbling blocks to positive therapeutic outcome should be "red flagged" immediately at the outset of treatment in any clinical assessments, diagnostic summaries, impairment profiles, patient outcome objectives, treatment objectives, or the like, sent to case managers and review specialists.

Questions that the therapist might ask the client that can aid in this determination process are:

"When did you first become aware of this symptom/problem?"

"Did someone else bring this problem/symptom to your attention or did you recognize this problem/symptom on your own?"

"Was the decision to seek professional assistance with this problem/symptom your own decision or were you advised or ordered to seek counseling by someone else, such as an employer, supervisor, spouse, or parent?"

If the client was indeed sent to treatment by another individual or agency, the therapist should try to evaluate his/her motivation for change. One technique that may be helpful is to ask the client to rate how important change really is to him/her. For example, the client can be asked to complete this simple rating scale:

1. To what degree does this symptom/problem bother you? *(Circle one)*

Not at all bothersome   *Extremely bothersome*

1   2   3   4   5   6   7   8   9   10

2. How important is it for you *personally* that this symptom/problem be reduced significantly? *(Circle one)*

Not at all important   *Extremely important*

1   2   3   4   5   6   7   8   9   10

3. How important is it for you *personally* that this symptom/problem be eliminated completely? *(Circle one)*

Not at all important   *Extremely important*

1   2   3   4   5   6   7   8   9   10

The client then is asked to rate the same three questions as he/she believes his/her employer, supervisor, parent, or spouse (i.e., the person who sent him/her for treatment) would rate them.

1. To what degree do you believe this symptom is bothersome to your _____ (employer, supervisor, parent, spouse, etc.)? (Fill in person's name and/or relationship to client.) *(Circle one)*

   Not at all bothersome   *Extremely bothersome*

   1   2   3   4   5   6   7   8   9   10

2. How important do you believe reducing your symptom/problem significantly is to your _____ ? *(Circle one)*

   Not at all important   *Extremely important*
      for him/her   *for him/her*

   1   2   3   4   5   6   7   8   9   10

3. How important do you believe completely eliminating your symptom/problem is to your _____ ? *(Circle one)*

   Not at all important   *Extremely important*
      for him/her   *for him/her*

   1   2   3   4   5   6   7   8   9   10

Finally, the client is asked to make the following four ratings:

1. To what degree is maintaining your current job dependent on a significant reduction in your symptom/problem? *(Circle one)*

   Not at all dependent   *Critical and necessary*

   1   2   3   4   5   6   7   8   9   10

2. To what degree is maintaining your current job dependent on the complete elimination of your symptom/problem? *(Circle one)*

   Not at all dependent   *Critical and necessary*

   1   2   3   4   5   6   7   8   9   10

3. To what degree is maintaining your marriage (relationship with partner) dependent on a significant reduction in your symptom/problem behavior? *(Circle one)*

Not at all dependent   *Critical and necessary*

1   2   3   4   5   6   7   8   9   10

4. To what degree is maintaining your marriage (relationship with partner) dependent on the complete elimination of your symptom/problem behavior? *(Circle one)*

Not at all dependent   *Critical and necessary*

1   2   3   4   5   6   7   8   9   10

The answers to these simple questions not only furnish the therapist with some pertinent information about the client's possible motives for entering treatment at this time and his/her motivation for change, but they also supply the therapist with some preliminary data about the need for collateral contacts in the future and with whom these contacts might be appropriate. It is important that case managers, review specialists, etc., be informed, as early as possible, about the possible or probable need for collateral involvements so that the approval process can begin.

If the client has made the decision to seek professional assistance voluntarily, and has not been urged (or forced) into treatment by a third party, a detailed history of the presenting problem is the next order of business. This should not be confused with the traditional history-taking interviews that psychoanalysts, psychiatrists, psychologists, and social workers routinely conduct. These interviews were designed to gather genetic information about early childhood experiences and their possible influences on personality development and symptom formation. The problem-focused interview is much narrower in scope. It is primarily concerned with gathering information that is *relevant to the resolution of the client's presenting problem and/or to the successful modification of specific symptoms/behaviors.*

As was mentioned earlier, the problem's duration is something that must be considered before a viable treatment plan can be devised. If the therapist finds that the client's problem does have a long-standing, chronic, and/or recurrent history, this information should not be taken to mean that any treatment attempt will be doomed to failure. It does mean, however, that some time must be spent with the client in formulating treatment goals and defining behavioral outcomes that are realistically achievable in the time frame and/or number of sessions that are available under the client's managed mental health care contract.

Another consideration is whether the *frequency of the problem behavior* has changed over the course of its history. Increased frequency and/or exacerbation of symptoms, problem behaviors, etc., often mean that something, someone, or some current circumstance is directly involved in the problem's worsening and/or the client's deterioration. A thorough *situational* analysis will help the therapist and client identify possible causes and contributing factors. Questions that will be helpful in this discernment process include:

In what situations, environments, and interpersonal contexts does the symptom/problem behavior occur?

Most frequently?
Least frequently?
Never?

In what situations, environments, and interpersonal contexts is the symptom/problem behavior:

Most severe?
Least severe?

What can the client identify as antecedent cues or stimuli that set off the problem behavior or cause the symptom to appear?

What people serve as antecedent cues or stimuli?

What thoughts, internal monologues, etc., is the client aware of that might serve as antecedent cues or stimuli?

What perceptions, attributions, and expectations about specific people, places, things, etc., does the client believe serve as antecedent cues and discriminative stimuli for the appearance of the symptom or the occurrence of the problem behavior under consideration?

It is important during this very early stage of treatment that the therapist teach the client how to think about and conceptualize his/

her problem in behaviorally explicit language that will make it possible to devise a concrete and detailed intervention program. Once the client is able to do this, a similar analysis of his/her cognitions, feelings, internal dialogues, perceptions, attributions, and so forth is then undertaken to determine which of these factors might be fueling the symptom/problem behavior as it is actually being exhibited.

Next, a similar analysis of these factors is conducted to determine what thoughts, feelings, people, situations, interpersonal contexts, cues, and reinforcing stimuli can be identified as serving to maintain the symptom or problem behavior. Finally, the same procedure is used to determine what people, thoughts, feelings, and behavioral consequences have been effective in reducing or inhibiting (temporarily) the appearance, frequency, or severity of the symptom or problem behavior.

The final aspect of any situation analysis is to help the client reflect upon the pragmatic outcomes or consequences of his/her behavior for himself/herself and for significant others who are intimately involved and directly affected by the symptom or behavior under observation.

The client should also be asked to consider, carefully, any additional factors or bits of information that might be related to the initiation, maintenance, or reduction of the troublesome symptom/behavior.

The situational analysis is an excellent way to discover what persons are intimately involved with the symptom/problem behavior and its maintenance and without whose participation treatment would be of little value. Once key persons are identified, the following questions are in order:

What does this person do, say, etc., that serves as a stimulus cue for the appearance of the symptom or the exhibition of the problem behavior?

What does this person do, say, etc., that serves to maintain the symptom or problem behavior?

What does this person do, say, etc., to inhibit the symptom or the appearance of the problem behavior?

Does the client beneficiary believe that involving this person in therapy would be helpful in modifying the symptom/problem behavior and/or resolving the presenting problem?

This last question raises some very important professional, ethical, and legal issues that any therapist working for a managed mental health care corporation should consider. For example, if the situational analysis reveals or the client specifically indicates that his/ her symptom, problem behavior, etc., is directly related to involvement with a spouse, family member, sibling, or parent, the therapist should know that the treatment of record for such relationship difficulties is marital or family intervention (depending on what significant family members are identified as being involved with the problem). Furthermore, the therapist should also know that to withhold this information from the client and to proceed to treat the client individually without involving relevant family members would probably violate most professional codes of ethics.

If collateral contacts are not approved for the treatment of such problems or conditions, the therapist has the responsibility to inform the client (a) that the treatment approved by the managed mental health care company is *not* the treatment of choice, (b) that the treatment sanctioned by the managed mental health company may have detrimental effects on the client's marriage or family system, and (c) that there are other treatments that he/she should explore and consider before agreeing to participate in individual therapy. However, giving clients all this information may still not absolve the therapist. Some legal scholars have argued that when the treatment of choice is denied to a client by a managed mental health care organization, the therapist must act on the client's behalf and become the client's advocate vis-à-vis the managed mental health care company. Not to do so may be considered negligence on the therapist's part—an action for which the therapist may be liable (Appelbaum, 1993).

2

Individual Diagnoses and Marital/Family Assessment: A Complementary Process

It is important not to lose sight of the fact that marital and family interventions are seen as *adjuncts to individually focused treatments* and that collateral contacts with other family members are approved only for a specific number of sessions by most managed mental health care organizations. This reality, however, should not be disheartening to marriage and family therapists since marriage and family therapies, as originally conceptualized by pioneering systems therapists, were seen as treatments of short duration (Haley, 1963; Jackson, 1959; Watzlawick, Beavin, & Jackson, 1967).

The goal of these newly devised systems interventions was to interrupt and modify homeostatic marital and family interaction sequences and structural configurations that were believed to be maintaining the identified patient's symptom or problem behavior. Since the system or problem itself was also seen as a major focus that served to maintain the dysfunctional family pattern, interventions had to be devised that would disrupt these processes and structures quickly, thus enabling the system to recalibrate at a higher and more viable level of functioning. Brief and short-term treatments, therefore, are in keeping with both the letter and the spirit of systems-based therapies as originally conceptualized and practiced.

Therefore, one would expect all therapists who request approval for collateral contacts with family members for the purpose of brief

11

or short-term family systems intervention to have had supervised training in brief and short-term, problem-focused, behavioral systems approaches to solving marital and family problems, as well as being formally trained to use structural, strategic, and functional models of marital/family intervention when these are deemed to be appropriate. Much more will be said about issues of training and preparation for brief and short-term therapies in Chapter 8.

Once it is determined that collateral contacts are appropriate, the selection of instruments and assessment procedures for both individual diagnosis and marital or family assessment is the next step in the process. It does not matter whether the instruments or procedures selected for diagnosis and evaluation are designed for use with individuals, marriages, or family systems; *there are certain issues that must be taken into account before one proceeds*. These are listed below.

ISSUES IN SELECTING INSTRUMENTS

Validity Considerations

Is the instrument, assessment device, procedure, etc., a valid measure of what it purports to measure? Were appropriate methodological and statistical procedures used to establish validity?

Reliability Considerations

Is the instrument, assessment device, procedure, etc., consistent? Is it dependable? Were appropriate methodological and statistical procedures used to establish reliability?

Universal Applicability

Is this instrument, assessment device, procedure, etc., applicable to work with a wide variety of clients (e.g., age groups, sexes, ethnic minorities, racial groups, social classes)?

Theory–Practice Considerations

To what extent was a coherent, recognized, and accepted theory of individual, marital, or family behavior used as a guide for constructing this particular instrument, assessment device, procedure, etc.? To what extent do client responses to this instrument or the findings gleaned from this assessment process lend themselves to the development of a behaviorally specific intervention strategy? How do scores on this instrument, procedure, or the like translate into meaningful treatment goals?

Sensitivity to Clinical Change

How sensitive is this instrument, device, procedure, etc., to detecting changes in the client's actual behaviors, feelings, cognitions, etc., that result from planned intervention? Does the instrument or procedure detect small and subtle changes or is it sensitive only to gross and global changes in the client's behaviors, cognitions, affects, etc.?

Expertise and Training

Can the instrument, device, or procedure be used by most practitioners, or does utilization require the therapist to have had highly specialized training, extensive preparation, considerable clinical experience, or prolonged supervision before being able to interpret and utilize test findings independently? To what extent is subjective interpretation or clinical inference used to make assessments, clinical evaluations, diagnoses, and so forth?

Overall Costs

When one is estimating the costs involved in using any assessment instrument or diagnostic procedure, the actual purchase price represents only one factor. The time required for (a) administration, (b) scoring, (c) interpretation, (d) giving feedback to clients, (e) developing mutually agreed upon treatment goals, and (f) devising a concrete behaviorally specific treatment plan to achieve these goals must be taken into account when one is considering overall costs.

In a very real sense, time spent in managed mental health care is money spent. Therefore, valid and reliable instruments that can be administered easily and scored quickly by practitioners would be most appropriate for managed mental health care practice. Similarly, instruments and procedures that facilitate the identification of specific behaviors that then can become the focus of treatment are ideal for managed mental health care. Some guidelines for instrument selection are presented in the next section.

INDIVIDUAL MEASURES AND MARITAL/FAMILY ASSESSMENT: SOME CONCEPTUAL ISSUES

Evaluating the individual functioning of both spouses or all relevant family members does not mean that a system-oriented therapist must abandon the systems orientation, since individual measures can be extremely helpful in determining how couples and family members function as interrelated components of a larger system (Bagarozzi, 1985; Bagarozzi & Anderson, 1989; L'Abate & Bagarozzi, 1993). Early systems theorists were behavioral and pragmatic in their work with couples and families (Bateson, 1935, 1936, 1972; Haley, 1963; Watzlawick, Beavin, & Jackson, 1967). They believed that all behavior exhibited by an individual is communication and that one could not *not* communicate.

In addition, they said that all communication–behavioral exchanges were either symmetrical or complementary. Symmetrical behaviors are behaviors that are identical or similar in nature. For example, if a spouse or family member exhibits a hostile or aggressive behavior and the individual to whom this behavior is directed responds in kind, that is, with an equally (or more severe) hostile or aggressive response, the behavioral exchange shared by these two family members would be considered symmetrical. If a husband is depressed and behaves in an apathetic manner, a symmetrical response would be for his wife also to become depressed and apathetic. A woman who has an extramarital affair in order to retaliate against her husband for his infidelity is also engaging in a symmetrical exchange. Finally, a husband who responds to his wife's erotic advances with his own sexual arousal is engaging in a symmetrical behavior exchange.

Complementary behavioral exchanges, on the other hand, are behavioral reciprocations that are logically opposite. For example, the fearful submission of a spouse to his/her mate's threats would be considered a complementary response. Increased depression in response to another family member's attempt to cheer up a depressed person and a husband's calm and rational response to his wife's panic attack are further examples of behavioral complementarity.

If one accepts this systems interpretation of behavior, the assessment of the identified patient's symptom or problem behavior is meaningful only if all other family members are evaluated along the same dimensions, as well as their logical opposites.

In 1973, a team of researchers identified a third type of relational communication interaction pattern, which they called "parallel" (Ericson & Rogers, 1973). Parallel interactions are characterized by reciprocal exchanges of different (as opposed to identical or opposite) behaviors. Parallel responses are also thought to be more functionally flexible than either symmetrical or complementary exchanges and are believed to represent a higher logical order of responding. These findings have important implications for the practice of brief and short-term marital and family therapies and will be discussed in detail in the treatment chapters that follow. At this time, however, let us return to the discussion of how individual measures can be used to investigate complementary and symmetrical processes in marital and family systems.

For the purpose of this discussion, let us say that a client comes in for an initial individual interview and identifies his major problem as "feeling low, down, tired, and depressed lately." After completing a thorough history of the presenting problem, the therapist determines that the client's depression is a recent phenomenon, not a chronic or recurring problem. The therapist also learns that the client has come to counseling at his wife's insistence. Finally, the therapist determines that the first signs of the client's depression appeared in the form of loss of appetite, irritability, and an inability to fall asleep at night. These symptoms of depression became evident soon after his youngest child (the last child to leave home) moved to his own apartment.

In order to assess the degree and severity of the client's depression and his suicidal potential, the therapist asks him to complete the Beck Depression Inventory (Beck, 1978) and the Suicidal Ideation Questionnaire (Reynolds, 1991). Based on the therapist's clinical interview and the client's score on the Suicidal Ideation Questionnaire, the therapist judges the client not to be a suicidal risk. However, his score on the Beck Depression Inventory indicates a significant degree of depression, which supports the therapist's own clinical appraisal of the symptom's severity.

Based on the information gathered in the initial interview and the client's scores on these two measures, the therapist makes a request for collateral sessions with the client's wife and his youngest son, who had recently left home.

In the first collateral contact, both the spouse and the son are asked to complete the Beck Depression Inventory (Beck, 1978) and some brief marital (for the wife only) as well as assessment instruments that the therapist deems appropriate. Much more will be said about the selection and use of appropriate marital and family measures throughout this volume, but for the purpose of this discussion, only the scores on the Beck Depression Inventory will be dealt with to illustrate the concept of the symmetrical and complementary nature of symptomatic behavior.

Let us now assume that the therapist finds that neither the wife nor the son have any significant degree of depression. As a matter of fact, the therapist observes that both wife and son spend a considerable amount of time actively trying to draw the identified patient out of his depression. Their upbeat attempts to involve the patient are complementary to his inactivity and depression. The more depressed the identified patient becomes, the more time both wife and son spend trying to bring him out of his depression. This only reinforces his depressed mood and behavior.

If, on the other hand, the therapist were to find that the wife and the son both scored high on the Beck Depression Inventory and that all three family members exhibit depressed behavior in the family session, this would be an excellent example of behavioral symmetry. The therapist might then speculate about the meaning of this family group depression. For example, (a) depression represents this family's characteristic mood and tone (Lewis, Beavers, Gossett, & Phillips, 1976; (b) depression is a temporary, yet typical, response to separation in this family; (c) the family has an unverbalized rule that love, affection, and caring can be demonstrated only via painful communication channels (Strayhorn, 1978); (d) depression is symptomatic of a significant theme in this family's mythology (Bagarozzi & Anderson, 1989); (e) family cohesion is maintained through depression; or (f) the family is struggling with issues having to do with unresolved loss and mourning.

Finally, let us assume that the therapist finds the wife to be depressed, but that the son's scores indicate no significant degree of depression. This would be an example where both complementary and symmetrical patterns exist. In my clinical experience, I have found this latter pattern to be the most common. When this type of arrangement is discovered, the therapist must try to understand how these dyadic patterns fit together and how the various pattern combinations work together to stabilize the larger family system.

Further Systems Considerations

Haley (1963) described, in great detail, how the symptomatic behavior of one spouse often protects the partner and the marriage. In such cases, the symptom of the identified patient has become integrated with the symptom of the nonsymptomatic spouse in a way that conceals that spouse's symptoms. For example, a claustrophobic woman's fear of enclosed places makes it impossible for her to ride in elevators. However, her claustrophobia protects her husband from having to deal with his own fear of high places. I once treated a woman whose agoraphobia made it impossible for her husband to take overnight trips out of town. When the two were seen together, however, it became evident that the husband frequently experienced panic attacks when he was separated from his wife.

Haley (1963) believes that it is impossible for one spouse to have a severe symptom without the symptom of the mate being an integral part of the couple's relationship even though the operative aspects of the symptom may not be readily apparent. If one accepts this systemic view of the interrelated nature of symptoms, individual treatment is futile.

The implications of this theoretical orientation for the practice of psychotherapy in the context of managed mental health care are clear. *The number of treatment sessions can be reduced when the spouse of a symptomatic client beneficiary actively participates in the treatment process.*

Some Additional Couple Dynamics

Acting out is a psychoanalytic term that refers to a person's unconscious reproduction of repressed conflicts, feelings, memories, and so on in his/her behavior with others who represent significant figures from the past. This type of behavior is called transference acting out and should not be confused with the popular misuse of the term "acting out" to describe any antisocial activity or undesirable behavior. In psychoanalytic theory, acting out is always an attempt to re-create, relive, and resolve unconscious childhood conflicts and trauma in the present through interactions with transference figures.

In intimate relationships with spouses, family members, lovers, or close friends, a different type of acting out—*collusive acting out for a significant other*—frequently occurs. In collusive acting out, one person unwittingly acts out the repressed, unconscious, and unacceptable desires, wishes, impulses, conflicts or split-off parts of the self for another. Collusive acting out is more easily identifiable in family systems where a child acts out the unconscious wishes or impulses, for instance, of one or both parents (Bagarozzi & Anderson, 1989). However, collusive acting out between adult partners is more difficult to identify.

Case Example

I once saw a middle-aged man who was referred to me for individual treatment by his employer. The client was a slightly built, neatly groomed, and well-mannered man. I was surprised to learn that he had been referred to me because he had had some minor clashes with his supervisor for which he had received a letter of reprimand for insubordination.

A history of the presenting problem revealed that the client had been terminated from two previous positions because of his verbal abuse of subordinates and co-workers. Insubordination, however, was a more recent development. Verbal abuse of subordinates and co-workers had begun shortly after the client's marriage. Prior to that, there had been no incidents of verbal abuse in the workplace.

In order to get a more rounded picture of the problem, I asked the client if I could confer with his supervisors, and he gave me permission to do so. The supervisors with whom I spoke both agreed that the client was an excellent and dependable worker but that he had a tendency to become verbally abusive. Neither supervisor could identify what might be causing the client to behave abusively. The men with whom he had come into conflict were characterized as being productive workers who had no prior histories of job-related conflicts. Neither supervisor could understand why the client would abuse two "model employees." The supervisor who cited the client for insubordination was genuinely puzzled by his behavior, but indicated that the client risked termination if his behavior was not brought under control.

In the next individual interview, I spent a considerable amount of time reviewing the client's thoughts, attributions, attitudes, perceptions, and internal dialogues that occurred prior to, during, and immediately following his verbal and emotional outbursts with his co-workers and supervisor in order to determine if I had overlooked anything of significance during the initial interview. The theme of these cognitions was clear and remained the same. Phrases such as "I won't let him get the best of me," "I'm a man just like he is," "I'm no pushover," and "I won't roll over and play dead for anybody" often served as stimulus cues that fueled his anger. Thoughts that immediately followed his outbursts were: "I guess I showed you," "You can't push me around," and "I'm no wimp."

I then asked the client if he would bring his wife in for the next interview so that I could get her perspective on things. I added that since his job was in jeopardy, "We could use all the help we could get."

The conjoint interview with this man's spouse proved to be enlightening. This was the second marriage for her. She had divorced her first husband because she considered him a "wimp." She said that in her first marriage her husband had been exploited by his employers, but he never "stood up for himself." She referred to herself as the one who "really wore the pants in that marriage." When asked about her current husband's difficulties at his place of employment and her feelings about his situation, she said that she was proud of his ability to "take care of himself" and "not get pushed around."

The key to the man's difficulties at his job was his relationship with his wife. His acting out of her wishes, desires, and unresolved conflicts and her reinforcement of his acting out in the workplace became the focus of therapy. Teaching this client how to be appropriately assertive with his co-workers, supervisors, and employer (as opposed to being hostile, aggressive, abusive, and belligerent) *was only possible if his wife agreed with this goal and actively participated in the training sessions and reinforced her husband for his newly acquired skills.*

In this instance, as in most cases where collateral contacts are warranted, the number of overall sessions can be reduced. Collateral contacts should be seen in this light; that is, *they are used to enhance and accelerate the treatment process and not to prolong it.*

The reader will notice that in this last example the reinforcing agent responsible for maintaining the problem was not identified in the initial interview through the questions designed to assess the client's motivation and commitment to change. The client was not extremely bothered by his problem behavior although his employer and supervisor were. Even though his job was in jeopardy, this still did not appear to be a strong enough incentive for change. His wife was not cited as a person urging him to change his behavior. As a matter of fact, she was described as supportive and understanding. Their marital happiness was not thought to be dependent on the client's keeping his current job.

As a rule of thumb, it is always wise to explore as many interpersonal systems as possible in order to identify what relationship systems might be contributing to the maintenance and perpetuation of the client's symptom/problem behavior. It might be helpful to think of this assessment in terms of a situational–contextual bull's-eye with the client at its center; the ever-widening concentric circles represent larger and larger interpersonal–contextual systems, as shown in Figure 1.

Thinking about intervention in this way is especially helpful when one finds that the treatment plan is not producing the desired results. At such times, it is helpful to review the bull's-eye in order to see what interpersonal systems and contexts, previously assessed, might require further investigation.

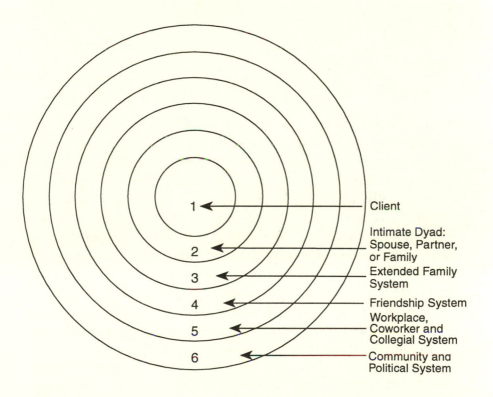

1 — Client

2 — Intimate Dyad: Spouse, Partner, or Family

3 — Extended Family System

4 — Friendship System

5 — Workplace, Coworker and Collegial System

6 — Community and Political System

Figure 1. Situational–contextual bull's-eye.

3

Choosing Appropriate Assessment Instruments for Marital and Family Intervention

REFINEMENT IN THE ASSESSMENT PROCESS

The family systems complex is comprised of four interrelated levels of functioning, which correspond to the first three circles in Figure 1 on the preceding page: (1) the individual (identified patient/client beneficiary), (2) the marital dyad/parental subsystem and the nuclear family (including all children from previous relationships who are currently living in the couple's home), and (3) the extended family system and kinship network (including all children from previous relationships who do not reside with the nuclear family, as well as divorced spouses, former in-laws, and children's grandparents, godparents, etc., from previous marriages).

Once the therapist has determined which individuals from what levels of systems functioning are intimately involved in the presenting problem and the maintenance of it, the issue becomes one of deciding whether it is feasible and desirable to involve these individuals directly in the treatment as collateral contacts. For example, an executive I treated for depression shared custody of her two preadolescent children with her former husband. This very efficient and conscientious woman would arrange out-of-town business trips only during times when her children were scheduled to visit their father. On a number of occasions, however, her former husband unilaterally canceled the children's visitations. These cancellations were often made on the night before the woman was scheduled to leave town. On two occasions, his abrupt cancellations made it impossible for this woman to follow through on her business commitments. These incidents produced negative consequences for her, her superiors, and the corporation that employed her.

This client's depression was related to her inability to be assertive and direct with her former husband. Her divorce from him took a great deal of courage, but she still had not fully mastered being assertive and straightforward with him. Although this woman's depression was related to her inability to set limits with her former husband, it would have been inappropriate to involve him directly in her treatment. Assertiveness training made it possible for the client to negotiate her differences with her former husband. Her depression began to lift, and her relationship with her superiors improved. Collateral contacts and the direct involvement of the former husband, however, were not necessary to produce the desired therapeutic outcomes.

When it is decided that other family members should be included in the treatment, the therapist must consider which of the valid and reliable instruments available for use are *the most appropriate for assessing this specific problem for this particular family at this point in the family system's development* (e.g., socioeconomic; ethnic, racial, religious factors, and family life-cycle stages considerations).

It is helpful to think of the assessment process as one of continual refinement, the goal of which is behavioral specificity. It is essential, therefore, for the therapist to be familiar with problem-specific instruments and procedures that can be used to concretize and further refine treatment goals. For example, if a client seeks help for a sexual problem, it would be important for the therapist assigned to treat that client to be able to conduct a sexual history/history of the sexual problem interview (L'Abate & Bagarozzi, 1992). Furthermore, the therapist assigned to such a case should be conversant with what assessment instruments are available for further refinement once specific problems or issues are identified.

For example, if the sexual history/history of the sexual problem interview reveals that the client's difficulties stem from faulty, incomplete, or inaccurate sex education, the therapist should be aware of those instruments that can be used to clarify the problem further, such as the Sex Education Liberalism Scale (Libby, 1971), the Sex Knowledge Inventory (Digran & Anspaugh, 1978), and the Sex-Love-Marriage Association Scale (Weis, Slosnerick, Cate, & Sollie, 1986).

If, however, the sexual history/history of the sexual problem interview reveals that the client suffers from a severe sexual inhibition, the therapist should be familiar with those assessment instruments that can help pinpoint the source or sources of the inhibition; for example, the Sexual Irrationality Questionnaire (Jordan & McCormick, 1988), Mosher Guild Inventory (Mosher, 1966, 1968), Sex Anxiety Inventory (Janda & O'Grady, 1980), Sexual Orientation Method and Anxiety Questionnaire (Patterson & O'Gorman, 1986), Sexual Anxiety Scale (Obler, 1973), Sexual Attitudes and Beliefs Inventory (Schiavi, Derogatis, Kuriansky, O'Connor, & Sharpe, 1979), and the Internalized Shame Scale (Cook, 1989).

Based on the information gathered from the sexual history/history of the sexual problem interview and one or more of the instruments cited above, the therapist can determine whether collateral contacts and joint sessions with the client's spouse are appropriate.

Similarly, let us suppose that a client requests help with difficulties that stem from unresolved conflicts with parents and/or siblings. The therapist should be familiar with those assessment instruments that make it possible to isolate salient intergenerational problems and sibling relationship issues so that they can be dealt with in therapy. Examples include the Family-of-Origin Scale (Hovestadt, Anderson, Piercy, Cochran, & Fine, 1985), the Personal Authority in the Family Systems Questionnaire (Bray, Williamson, & Malone, 1984), and the Sibling Systems Scale (Yourglich, 1966).

By using instruments such as these, the therapist can more easily identify key persons in the client's family of origin who are intimately involved in the presenting problem and the maintenance of it. Once this has been accomplished, the therapist can determine (with the client) whether the involvement of key family members is necessary or whether the intergenerational or sibling difficulties identified through assessment refinement can be resolved through short-term counseling/psychotherapy, reeducation, goal-specific training, or carefully constructed intergenerationally focused homework assignments that are specifically designed to treat and resolve the presenting problem or problems.

ASSESSMENT OF THE MARITAL DYAD

When a client's presenting problem is clearly a marital one, the economic treatment of choice is marital therapy/marriage counseling, and both spouses must be present and motivated to improve their relationship if brief or short-term counseling is to be effective (Gurman, Kniskern, & Pinsof, 1986). In my clinical work with distressed relationships, I usually conduct a comprehensive marital assessment (Bagarozzi & Anderson, 1989). This diagnostic and assessment process usually consists of a series of interviews, homework assignments, in-session tasks, and behavioral enactments. Typically, six clinical interviews are needed just to complete the assessment process alone. The usual procedure is described in the following sections.

The Marital Session

The couple is seen together and each spouse is asked to describe what he/she considers to be the presenting problem. The spouses are then asked to discuss what they have done, in the past, to resolve this particular difficulty. Next, they are asked to demonstrate, for the therapist, how they usually attempt to discuss this problem and resolve their conflict. They are given 10 minutes to carry out this assignment. Their conflict resolution attempts are videotaped.

After the couple has completed this assignment, each spouse is given a battery of assessment instruments to complete in private. The spouses are asked not to confer with each other or to discuss their answers. They are told that their responses to all questionnaires, instruments, and so on will be used to develop a marital relationship diagnostic profile that will allow the therapist to identify the strengths and weaknesses in their marriage and the general areas of distress and conflict that require attention. The spouses are also told that they will be able to read and review their partner's responses to all questions and that these instruments will be used throughout the therapeutic process to help them identify and resolve the critical issues of concern that brought them in for consultation.

Some of the instruments routinely used for marital assessment include:

MARITAL SATISFACTION MEASURES

1. Locke-Wallace Marital Adjustment Scale (Locke & Wallace, 1959)
2. Dyadic Adjustment Scale (Spanier, 1976)

MARITAL DIAGNOSTIC MEASURES

1. Family Adaptability and Cohesion Scale III: Couple Version (Olson, Portner, & Lavee, 1985)
2. Family Environment Scale (Moos & Moos, 1981)
3. Intimacy Needs Survey (Bagarozzi, 1990)
4. Spousal Inventory of Desired Changes and Relationship Barriers: SIDCARB (Bagarozzi, 1983b)
5. Comprehensive Areas of Change Questionnaire (Mead, Vatcher, Wyne, & Roberts, 1990)

CRITICAL ISSUES MEASURES

1. The Conflict Tactics Scale (Straus, 1979)
2. Exchange Orientation Inventory (Murstein, Cerreto, & MacDonald, 1977)

The couple's videotaped conflict negotiation and problem resolution attempts are reviewed later by the therapist. Their interactions are subjected to analyses. The most frequently used coding systems and rating scales are:

1. The Beavers Interactional Scales (Beavers, Hampson, & Hulgus, 1985)
2. Marital Interaction Coding System (Weiss & Summers, 1983)
3. Relational Communication Coding System (Ericson & Rogers, 1973)
4. Functional Communication and Conflict Negotiation Adequacy Checklist (Bagarozzi, 1980b)

Individual Sessions

At the conclusion of the first marital interview, two additional individual diagnostic and assessment interviews are scheduled for each spouse. These additional sessions are used to gather a detailed history of the presenting problem that reflects each spouse's unique perceptions and perspectives. A detailed personal history is also taken by the therapist, and any relevant information that will allow the therapist to arrive at a tentative DSM-IV diagnosis is gathered. Based on this tentative diagnosis, appropriate individually focused assessment instruments and diagnostic aids are selected and administered.

Each spouse is informed that all material disclosed during these individual interviews is confidential and will not be shared with his/her mate.

Marital Feedback Session

Based on the material gathered in the previous conjoint and individual sessions, the couple is presented with the therapist's assessment findings. These are discussed in detail with the couple and any questions are answered straightforwardly by the therapist. The therapist then makes recommendations, and a mutually agreed on decision about the course or courses of action is reached (Bagarozzi, 1989).

A MODIFIED INTERVIEW SEQUENCE PROCEDURE
FOR MANAGED CARE PRACTICE

Obviously, a six-session marital/individual diagnostic and assessment series of clinical interviews, although thorough, would not be appropriate for work in most managed mental health care settings as they are currently structured. Typically, three to five collateral contacts with a spouse constitute the upper limit. Nevertheless, this does not mean that critical historical material can be neglected by managed care practitioners. What it does mean, however, is that very close attention must be given to the training and preparation of therapists who are to conduct these important interviews.

In order to ensure that the client-beneficiary receives the highest quality of care available within the total number of visits allowed under the terms of his/her managed mental health care contract, the therapist must be able to achieve three goals in the initial diagnostic interview, once it is determined that the presenting problem is definitely a marital one requiring collateral inclusion of the client's spouse.

The first goal is to arrive at an accurate, individual psychiatric diagnosis. The second is to gather as thorough a history of the relationship/marriage as time will permit. The third is to gather a detailed history of the marital problem.

Why Psychiatric Diagnoses?

Although there have been some family therapists who believe that psychiatric diagnoses belong to a different, if not incorrect, philosophical/clinical epistemology that is totally inappropriate for understanding and treating relationship systems (Dell, 1983; Keeney, 1982), the accurate diagnostic identification of certain psychiatric conditions is essential for pragmatic treatment planning and the successful practice of brief, time-limited, short-term, and problem-focused therapies that are the cornerstone of managed mental health care practice.

Accurate psychiatric diagnosis becomes even more important

when one considers the limited number of collateral sessions that are typically permitted under most managed mental health care contracts. The therapist practicing in a managed mental health care setting must be able to assess, usually within one or two diagnostic interviews, whether the client and his/her spouse are appropriate candidates for short-term, problem-focused behavioral marital intervention. Almost two decades ago, L'Abate (1976, 1977, 1981) outlined some very basic criteria for screening out individuals for whom time-limited, skills-training, educationally focused, and problem-centered relationship therapies would be inappropriate. The individual personality characteristics that L'Abate identified as problematic included:

1. Uncooperative, extremely hostile, angry, and explosive individuals who show high levels of mistrust and evidence the use of projective defenses, projective identification, scapegoating, and blaming.
2. Individuals with long-standing, entrenched psychosomatic disorders and delusional systems who externalize their conflicts.
3. Excessively defensive individuals who have very little capacity for taking personal responsibility for their own actions and who have a limited capacity for self-understanding and psychological insight.
4. Chaotic and disorganized individuals who have had a long history of failed interpersonal relationships and/or chronically conflicted marriages, especially, individuals who are involved in marriages in which they have been unable to (a) cooperate with their partners, (b) set mutually agreed-upon goals, and (c) carry out agreed-upon goals and previously negotiated roles, tasks, and responsibilities.
5. Individuals who expect a short-term structured experience to be a magical cure for long-standing personal problems and relationship difficulties.

The reader will recognize that in many instances individuals who exhibit such behaviors may be evidencing character traits that are symptomatic of severe personality disorders (e.g., antisocial, paranoid, passive-aggressive, explosive, inadequate, avoidant, narcissistic, and borderline). When the therapist suspects that one or both spouses has a serious characterological disturbance, it would be helpful to get some objective and independent confirmation through the use of a reliable and valid diagnostic test, such as the Minnesota Multiphasic Personality Inventory (MMPI). Confirmation of severe pathology is essential for realistic treatment planning, for making prognoses, and for evaluating treatment outcomes.

The History of the Couple's Relationship and Their Problem: Streamlined for Managed Care

Bagarozzi and Anderson (1989) developed two fairly long and comprehensive outlines that they use to gather information from each spouse about the history of the couple's relationship and the history of their presenting problem. A combined and condensed version of these two interviews has been designed for use in managed mental health care settings. With training and practice, a therapist should be able to gather all pertinent information about the history of the couple's relationship and the central problem within a 55-minute interview with each spouse. Questions included in this condensed version follow:

1. How did you meet your spouse?
2. What attracted you to your spouse?
3. Who initiated the dating process?
4. Who took the major responsibility for continuing the relationship and for moving it forward toward marriage?
5. What traits, behaviors, characteristics of your spouse did you find most attractive? Least attractive?
6. Did you live together before marriage?
7. Did you have sexual intercourse with your spouse before marriage?
8. Were you satisfied with your sexual relationship and were you orgasmic?
   (If the spouse identified a sexual problem at this juncture

and considers the sexual relationship to be the presenting problem, the therapist should conduct a sexual history/ history of the sexual problem (L'Abate & Bagarozzi, 1992). If the clinician is not a certified sex therapist, referral to a qualified sex therapist should be made.

9. Were there any significant circumstances in your personal life (e.g., death of a parent or significant other, illness of a parent or significant other, graduation from school, abusive home environment, personal illness, loss of employment, pregnancy) that you believe played an important part in your decision to marry the person you did or when to do so?

10. How did your respective parents react to your partner and your decision to marry?

11. How was the decision made concerning whether or not to have children and the number of children you were going to bring into the world as a couple?

12. When did you first notice that there was this particular problem in your relationship?

13. What have you done, as an individual, to correct this problem? What have you and your spouse done jointly, as a couple, to correct this problem?

14. What remedy or remedies have been successful in correcting this problem? What remedies have been unsuccessful?

15. What other significant people (e.g., family, friends, ministers, professionals) have been involved in the past or are now actively involved in trying to help you solve this problem?

16. How willing are you, on a scale of 1 to 10, to make changes in your own behavior so that this conflict or problem can be resolved successfully?

Not at all willing   *Very willing*

| 1 | 2 | 3 | 4 | 5 | 6 | 7 | 8 | 9 | 10 |

Based on information gathered by the therapist during each spouse's individual interview, a tentative diagnosis is arrived at for each spouse.* Brief, individually focused diagnostic aids and relevant marital assessment instruments are then selected and given to each spouse. Once all marital assessment aids have been completed and returned, they are scored by the therapist. A conjoint marital session is scheduled. During this session, the couple receives detailed and specific feedback from the therapist concerning the status of their relationship, its strengths, its weaknesses, major areas of conflict, and other relevant points. Any questions that the couple might have about these findings are answered by the therapist. At this juncture, the spouses are asked if they would like to proceed with short-term, problem-focused marital counseling/therapy for the purpose of resolving a particular problem or issue in their marriage. *If the couple decides to continue, the therapist helps them select one specific problem or conflict issue that they are both willing to work on for a specific number of sessions.*

The therapist then asks the couple to try to resolve their conflict over this particular problem in his/her presence. The couple is allowed five to seven minutes to complete this in-session task. The therapist observes their problem-solving and conflict-negotiation attempts and rates each spouse's performance on each of the following dimensions that make up the Functional Communication and Conflict Negotiation Adequacy Checklist (Bagarozzi, 1980b).

	Never	*Always*
1. Speaks directly to his/her partner.	1 2 3 4 5 6 7 8 9 10	
2. Looks at partner when speaking.	1 2 3 4 5 6 7 8 9 10	
3. Takes responsibility for his/her position and uses "I" statements.	1 2 3 4 5 6 7 8 9 10	

---

*If at this juncture in the assessment process the therapist has any questions about diagnoses, a standard psychological test, such as the MMPI, can be administered, or a psychiatric consultation may be arranged for the client or the spouse. Referral for a psychiatric evaluation is usually standard procedure for most managed mental health care organizations whenever the therapist believes that psychotropic medication may be required or when a client or spouse is considered to be a danger to himself/herself or to others and when there is evidence of active substance abuse.

	Never	*Always*

4. Is able to distinguish between thoughts and feelings and communicates these differences clearly to the partner.　1 2 3 4 5 6 7 8 9 10

5. Interrupts partner when he/she is speaking.　1 2 3 4 5 6 7 8 9 10

6. Attempts to "read" partner's mind.　1 2 3 4 5 6 7 8 9 10

7. Does not accept literal meaning of partner's statements, i.e., interprets them, finds hidden meaning in partner's statements.　1 2 3 4 5 6 7 8 9 10

8. Attributes malintention to partner's motives.　1 2 3 4 5 6 7 8 9 10

9. Attacks partner verbally.　1 2 3 4 5 6 7 8 9 10

10. Threatens partner.　1 2 3 4 5 6 7 8 9 10

11. Criticizes and puts down partner.　1 2 3 4 5 6 7 8 9 10

12. Ridicules partner.　1 2 3 4 5 6 7 8 9 10

13. Verbally or non-verbally disqualifies partner's statements or behaviors.　1 2 3 4 5 6 7 8 9 10

14. Verbally or non-verbally disconfirms partner's existence (e.g., ignores partner).　1 2 3 4 5 6 7 8 9 10

15. Blames partner.　1 2 3 4 5 6 7 8 9 10

16. Projects blame onto partner.　1 2 3 4 5 6 7 8 9 10

17. Triangulates others into the conflict.　1 2 3 4 5 6 7 8 9 10

18. Listens to partner when he/she is speaking.　1 2 3 4 5 6 7 8 9 10

	Never	*Always*
19. Tries to role take and see partner's perspective.	1 2 3 4 5 6 7 8 9 10	
20. Tries to be empathic and feel what partner is experiencing.	1 2 3 4 5 6 7 8 9 10	
21. Asks partner for clarification if what was said is not understood.	1 2 3 4 5 6 7 8 9 10	
22. Is able to paraphrase what partner has been saying (i.e., accurately hears partner's communication).	1 2 3 4 5 6 7 8 9 10	
23. Can identify a problem in behaviorally specific terms.	1 2 3 4 5 6 7 8 9 10	
24. Is able to recognize and state his/her contribution to the problem's maintenance.	1 2 3 4 5 6 7 8 9 10	
25. Can identify and propose behavioral alternatives for himself/herself that will correct the problem or resolve the particular issue.	1 2 3 4 5 6 7 8 9 10	

When the couple has completed this in-session assigned task, the therapist helps them perform a situational analysis of the targeted problem. This situational analysis is similar to the individual situational analysis outlined earlier. The major elements of this situational analysis for couples follow:

1. In what situations does this problem/conflict occur?
2. In what situations does the problem/conflict never occur?
3. In what situations is the problem/conflict most severe?
4. In what situations is the problem/conflict least severe?
5. What situations, people, thoughts, feelings, etc., set off the problem or create a conflict in your relationship?
6. How does each spouse behave in the midst of the problem/conflict?

7. How does each spouse feel at the time that the problem/conflict is taking place?
8. What does each spouse say to himself/herself at the time the problem/conflict is taking place?
9. How does each spouse behave toward the other during this time (i.e., what does each spouse say and do)?
10. How does each spouse feel about himself/herself, his/her partner, and the marriage whenever the problem behavior is exhibited or the conflict surfaces?
11. How does each spouse feel about himself/herself, his/her partner, and the marriage immediately after the conflict has ended?
12. What does each spouse feel and do later on, after having had a chance to think about what has happened?
13. What are the conditions in the couple's life and in their environment that each spouse believes contributes to maintaining their problem/conflict?
14. What are the conditions in the couple's life and in their environment that each spouse believes contributes (or can contribute) to reducing this particular problem behavior/relationship conflict?
15. What positive (reinforcing) behavior change strategies and tactics has each spouse used in the past that have been successful in reducing the conflict or solving this problem?
16. What negative (coercive, punishing, negatively reinforcing) behavior change tactics has each spouse used in the past to get his/her spouse to modify this problem behavior or to resolve this conflict?
17. Which of these tactics and strategies (both positive and negative) have been the most effective? Least effective?

If time permits, an incentive analysis can also be conducted. The key elements of an incentive analysis include the following questions:

1. What benefits would derive for each spouse if the problem behavior/conflict continued in its present form?

2. What benefits would derive for each spouse if the problem behavior/conflict got worse?
3. What benefits would come about for each spouse if the problem behavior/conflict were resolved satisfactorily?
4. What are the disadvantages for each spouse if the problem behavior/conflict continues in its present form or intensity?
5. What are the disadvantages for each spouse if the problem behavior/conflict becomes worse?
6. What are the disadvantages for each spouse if the problem behavior/conflict were resolved satisfactorily?

A final question that the therapist should ask the couple at the conclusion of the situational/incentive analysis is:

"Is there anything else about this problem/conflict that you think I should know that would assist me in helping you resolve this conflict?"

If the couple has sought professional assistance in the past for this problem or for other marital difficulties, the therapist should obtain written permission from each spouse to contact the couple's previous therapist or counselor to discuss their previous treatment, to obtain case notes and clinical summaries. If at all possible, the therapist should attempt to obtain this information before treatment goals are set and intervention strategies are planned.

The assessment procedure outlined makes it possible for the managed care therapist to gather relevant information about the history of the marriage and the history of the presenting problem, and so on, *through the use of only two collateral interviews.* Essentially, a diagnostic/assessment process that usually requires six interviews can be reduced to three one-hour sessions when therapists are properly trained.

MARITAL ASSESSMENT INSTRUMENTS: REFINEMENTS AND PRAGMATIC CONSIDERATIONS

Marital Satisfaction Measures

Although the two measures of marital satisfaction and adjustment discussed earlier, the Locke-Wallace Marital Adjustment Scale (Locke

& Wallace, 1959) and the Dyadic Adjustment Scale (Spanier, 1976), are short and concise, there is no practical reason for more than one valid and reliable instrument (measuring the same construct) to be used in managed mental health care work. The choice of a marital satisfaction/marital adjustment measure for managed mental health care purposes should be based on the following criteria: (a) its validity and reliability, (b) its brevity, and (c) its clinical utility. Both the Locke-Wallace Marital Adjustment Scale (Locke & Wallace, 1959) and the Dyadic Adjustment Scale (Spanier, 1976) meet the first two criteria, but fail to meet the third criterion, as they do not provide the therapist with a comprehensive overview of domains of marital interactions where potential conflicts and dissatisfactions often arise. In this sense, they are incomplete and ill suited for clinical practice in managed care.

The Locke-Wallace Marital Adjustment Scale (Locke & Wallace, 1959) takes approximately three to five minutes to complete, but covers only eight domains of married life (finances, recreation, affection, friendships, sexual relations, conventionality, philosophy of life, and in-laws). In addition to these domains, the Locke-Wallace asks spouses to rate their satisfaction with how they typically resolve marital conflicts, how they spend their leisure time, and their satisfaction with the degree to which they share and enjoy common interests. Several questions about marital trust are also included in this measure. Finally, spouses are asked to consider whether, in hindsight, they would still marry their current mates, marry a different person, or not marry at all.

The Dyadic Adjustment Scale (Spanier, 1976), on the other hand, requires that the respondents reflect more thoughtfully about their relationship. It takes a little longer to complete than does the Locke-Wallace as it contains, in addition to many of the same items, items that are unique to the Dyadic Adjustment Scale. Whereas the Locke-Wallace Scale is a global measure of marital adjustment, the Dyadic Adjustment Scale provides the therapist with a much more comprehensive picture of the relationship by breaking down marital adjustment into four empirically derived components: dyadic satisfaction, dyadic cohesion, dyadic consensus, and affectional expression. However, the Dyadic Adjustment Scale, in this author's opinion, does not offer the therapist any more clinically relevant information that can be used to set treatment goals than does the Locke-Wallace Marital Adjustment Scale.

The present author developed a simple measure of marital satisfaction (Bagarozzi, 1983b) that can be used for pretreatment/posttreatment evaluations in managed mental health care practice. It consists of two Likert-type questions:

		Not at all satisfied	*Very satisfied*
1. In general, how satisfied are you with your marriage?		1 2 3 4 5 6 7 8 9 10	
2. In general, how satisfied are you with your spouse?		1 2 3 4 5 6 7 8 9 10	

Bagarozzi found that the first question concerning satisfaction with one's spouse correlated significantly ($r = .71$, $p < .01$) with the total satisfaction score computed for the Locke-Wallace Marital Adjustment Scale (Locke & Wallace, 1959). The correlation for the second question ("In general, how satisfied are you with your spouse?") with the total Locke-Wallace satisfaction score was also significant ($r = .73$, $p < .01$). These empirical findings offer support for using the above two questions as valid pretreatment/posttreatment measures of therapeutic outcome in managed mental health care practice.

Later, Schumm, Jurich, and Bollman (1986) adopted these two questions as the basis for the development of their three-item Kansas Marital Satisfaction Scale:

1. How satisfied are you with your marriage?
2. How satisfied are you with your relationship with your husband (wife)?
3. How satisfied are you with your relationship with your husband (wife) as spouse?

However, Schumm, Jurich, and Bollman did not correlate these three items with the total satisfaction score of the Locke-Wallace Marital Adjustment Scale (Locke & Wallace, 1959). Therefore, it should not be used as a measure of marital satisfaction in managed mental health care practice at the present time.

Marital Diagnostic Measures

The Family Adaptability and Cohesion Scale III: FACES III (Olson, Portner, & Lavee, 1985) has been in use since 1978. Since its introduction into clinical literature, FACES has undergone a number of revisions (L'Abate & Bagarozzi, 1992). It was one of the first assessment tools that was developed to operationalize two central constructs of family systems theory, Adaptability and Cohesion.

FACES III, the shortest version of this instrument, consists of 20 items—10 for Cohesion and 10 for Adaptability. It can be completed in a minute or two and is easy to score. Olson, Portner, and Lavee (1985) stress the importance of administering FACES III twice (in both pretreatment and posttreatment sessions) in order to obtain each spouse's perceived and ideal description of his/her marriage. They believe that by comparing the perceived versus ideal discrepancies for each spouse, it is possible to assess each spouse's subjective level of marital satisfaction along these two dimensions of conjugal functioning.

Research into FACES III has shown the Cohesion dimension to have solid empirical support. Unfortunately, the same cannot be said for the Adaptability dimension of FACES III (Joanning & Kuehl, 1986). The brevity of FACES III for its Cohesion dimension is its major strength. Many couples seek marital counseling because they feel "alienated" from their spouses, or because the "intimacy" has gone out of their relationship. When "closeness" or "connectedness" in the marital dyad is the presenting problem, FACES III can be used as a global measure of marital quality and satisfaction for this one area of the relationship. However, for a more behaviorally specific refinement of difficulties in the area of marital intimacy, the Intimacy Needs Survey (Bagarozzi, 1990) can be used to clarify this presenting problem further.

The Intimacy Needs Survey was developed to help couples pinpoint those areas of intimacy where they feel unfulfilled. This clinical tool asks spouses to evaluate their satisfaction with eight separate dimensions of intimacy that are considered to constitute the larger construct of marital cohesion. These dimensions are emotional, psychological, intellectual, sexual, spiritual, aesthetic, social-recreational, and physical (nonsexual) intimacy. Three scores—(1) need strength, (2) satisfaction with a spouse's receptivity to one's felt and expressed intimacy needs, and (3) satisfaction with one's spouse's reciprocal disclosures of his/her intimacy needs—are computed. Reciprocal disclosure scores are computed for the first six dimensions. Only two scores (need strength and satisfaction with a spouse's receptivity to each of these needs) are computed for social-recreational intimacy and physical intimacy.

Since it takes about 12 minutes to score both spouses' Intimacy Needs questionnaires, the Intimacy Needs Survey should be administered in managed mental health care practice only when marital intimacy is the presenting problem. The therapist can then use the Intimacy Needs Survey (Bagarozzi, 1990) to help spouses pinpoint the specific aspects of intimacy where interventions should be focused.

Keeping in mind that reliability, validity, brevity, and clinical utility are all of paramount importance when it comes to selecting a pretreatment assessment instrument that clinicians can use in managed mental health care practice, we are faced with the task of finding a measure that will make it possible for a managed care therapist to investigate the broadest spectrum of marital behavior in the shortest time possible.

The Family Environment Scale (FES) (Moos & Moos, 1981) was developed to measure the social environmental characteristics of families. The scale is a 90-item, true/false, self-report measure that takes approximately five to seven minutes to complete. The scale assesses 10 dimensions of marriage, as opposed to FACES III, which deals only with two of these dimensions of marital/family life. These 10 dimensions are also grouped into three underlying domains:

I. *Relationship Domain*
   Cohesion
   Expressiveness
   Conflict

II. *Personal Growth Domain*
Independence
Achievement Orientation
Intellectual–Cultural Orientation
Active–Recreational Orientation
Moral–Religious Orientation

III. *Systems Maintenance Domain*
Organization
Control

The reader will note that two of the FACES III (Olson, Portner, & Lavee, 1985) dimensions, Cohesion and Control, are also included in the Family Environment Scale (Moos & Moos, 1981). In some instances when cohesion, closeness, intimacy, or the like are not the presenting problems, the Family Environment Scale may be used by seasoned marital and family therapists as a time-saving alternative to FACES III since it covers an additional eight dimensions and does not require much more time to complete. However, it is important to keep in mind that the Family Environment Scale is first and foremost a research instrument that was not meant to serve as a clinical assessment device. The major dimensions included in this scale are not derived from any recognizable theory of marital or family development, process, functioning, or therapy, and no guidelines exist for translating FES scores into specific treatment goals (L'Abate & Bagarozzi, 1992). Therefore, the utility of this scale as a clinical assessment tool for managed mental health care practice remains to be demonstrated. In this author's opinion, the Family Environment Scale does contribute valuable information about family environments and family values when used in conjunction with other theoretically based marital/family assessment instruments (Bagarozzi, 1989), but it cannot stand alone as a clinical tool to be used by managed mental health care practitioners.

In 1980, Stuart and Stuart published their Marital Precounseling Inventory. This exceptionally comprehensive questionnaire was composed of 13 separate subscales derived from 341 behaviorally worded items. This instrument required a considerable amount of time for completion and, therefore, was impractical for use in most clinical settings. The latest version of the Marital Precounseling Inventory (Stuart & Jacobson, 1991) still stands, in this author's opinion, as the most comprehensive marital assessment instrument available to date. Sadly, its length renders it unsuitable for managed mental health care practice in spite of its behaviorally focused format and clinical utility.

In an attempt to develop a brief, theoretically based, behaviorally focused and clinically useful assessment instrument for marital intervention, Bagarozzi (1983b) developed the Spousal Inventory of Desired Changes and Relationship Barriers: SIDCARB. This instrument is a 24-item Likert-style questionnaire that makes use of a seven-point response format. Specific response options vary according to the nature of each item. This scale was designed to tap into each spouse's perceptions of the conjugal/behavior exchange process. The first 10 items in Factor I assess satisfaction with the fairness in the marital exchange process in 10 central domains of marital relationships (i.e., household chores, finances, communication, expressions of love and of affection, recreation, sexual relations, friendships, in-laws, children, and religion). Items 11–15 assess overall satisfaction and commitment. Questions 18–24 operationalize the social exchange constructs of internal and external barriers to separation and divorce.

SIDCARB takes couples approximately three to five minutes to complete and can be scored in about the same amount of time. No special training is required for administration and scoring, but a theoretical understanding of social exchange theory is necessary for accurate clinical interpretation and treatment goal setting. This instrument has two additional drawbacks for use in managed mental health care practice. First, it is not a comprehensive measure since it does not assess all relevant domains of marriage. Second, SIDCARB was developed for use by clinicians who were trained in cognitive-behavioral approaches to marital therapy.

In this author's opinion, the pretreatment assessment instrument that offers the most promise for managed mental health care adoption is the comprehensive Areas of Change Questionnaire (Mead, Vatcher, Wyne, & Roberts, 1990). Based on the Areas of Change

Questionnaire developed by Weiss and Birchler (1983), the Comprehensive Areas of Change Questionnaire evaluates 16 categories of marital problems in addition to the 13 categories contained in the Weiss and Birchler (1983) version of this instrument. These 29 categories cover: (1) communication, (2) expectations, (3) affection, (4) loving feelings, (5) sex, (6) power struggles, (7) problem solving, (8) finances, (9) values, (10) roles, (11) children, (12) individual problems, (13) affairs, (14) household management, (15) in-laws, (16) conventionality, (17) jealousy, (18) employment, (19) leisure time, (20) alcoholism, (21) prior marriages, (22) psychosomatic illness, (23) friends, (24) addictions, (25) personal habit and personal appearance, (26) physical abuse, (27) religion, (28) health and physical handicaps, and (29) incest.

CRITICAL ISSUES MEASURES: REFINEMENTS AND PRACTICAL CONSIDERATIONS

The Exchange Orientation Inventory (Murstein, Cerreto, & MacDonald, 1977) is a theory-specific assessment instrument that can be effectively used as a screening device in clinical practice. Although not initially developed for clinical work, the Exchange Orientation Inventory enables the therapist to differentiate between individuals who view intimate relationships, such as marriage, in terms of equitable social exchanges and those for whom equity in the exchange process plays only a minor role in determining relationship satisfaction.

Since a social exchange (quid pro quo) format (Jackson, 1965; Jackson & Lederer, 1968) is one of the cornerstones of most brief and short-term marital therapies, and since the exchange of behaviors between spouses occupies a central role in the practice of virtually all behavioral approaches to resolving marital conflict, it is important for a therapist (not only a managed mental health care therapist) to know the degree to which each spouse uses exchange principles to make subjective judgments about his/her own marital satisfaction.

It has been this author's clinical experience that individuals who view their marriages in terms of social and behavioral exchanges are more comfortable negotiating behavioral marital contracts than are individuals who receive low scores on the Exchange Orientation Inventory (Murstein, Cerreto, & MacDonald, 1977). Knowing each spouse's exchange orientation can help a managed mental health care therapist decide the degree to which a behavioral exchange model of brief intervention should be used with a given couple.

Finally, videotaping couples and later scoring or rating their interactions is a procedure that requires a considerable amount of time, training, and expertise. Such assessments are cost-prohibitive for most managed mental health care practices. However, it is probably safe to assume that the majority of couples who are in need of marital therapy do not communicate well and would benefit from some type of communications skill training and problem-solving approaches to resolving marital conflicts. Therefore, there is really no reason to quantify dysfunctional interaction patterns by using coding systems or rating scales. These can be omitted from the assessment process. In their place, however, one may consider using the brief Conflict Tactics Scale (Straus, 1979) to get each spouse's perceptions concerning how differences of opinion and conflicts are typically handled in their marriage. The Conflict Tactics Scale assesses the frequency and degree to which each spouse uses three types of conflict resolution strategies to end marital disputes. The three tactics identified by Straus are verbal reasoning, verbal aggression, and physical aggression. This last category is broken down further into two subtypes: the use of lethal or nonlethal force.

When violence is found to be present in a marriage, appropriate steps must be taken by the therapist to put an end to it (Bagarozzi & Giddings, 1982, 1983). If the therapist assigned to the case has little experience working with domestic violence or has had no formal training in working with violent spouses, immediate referral to another therapist in the network who is skilled in this area should be made. In the event that no other therapist in the network has the requisite skills and training to deal with this issue, referral to a qualified out-of-network therapist or program is in order.

Two additional modifications in the couple assessment process discussed at the beginning of this chapter are the elimination of videotaping couples' interactions and the removal of the three time-consuming and cumbersome coding systems and rating scales—the Beavers Interactional Scales (Beavers, Hampson, & Hulgus, 1985), the Marital Interaction Coding System (Weiss & Summers, 1983), and the Relational Communication Coding System (Ericson & Rogers, 1973). In their place, the Functional Communication and Conflict Negotiation Adequacy Checklist (Bagarozzi, 1980b) can be used by the therapist while the couple is completing the conflict resolution task assigned by the therapist. This checklist, which is reproduced on pages 32–34, can be used by most marital therapists with little difficulty.

PRAGMATIC ASSESSMENT OF COUPLES

In 1992, Bagarozzi designed the Pragmatic Marital Assessment Questionnaire (Bagarozzi, 1992a) for use by therapists who were working in managed mental health care settings and who desired a quick and easy way to make *clinically meaningful* pretreatment assessments of couples seeking marriage counseling/marital therapy. The PMAQ, in its present form (shown below), is a clinical aid, the reliability and validity of which have yet to be established. Therefore, it should not be used by practitioners or managed mental health care organizations as a measure of accountability.

Pragmatic Marital Assessment Questionnaire

PART I

	Not at all satisfied	*Very satisfied*
1. In general, how satisfied are you with your spouse?	1 2 3 4 5 6 7 8 9 10	
2. In general, how satisfied are you with your marriage?	1 2 3 4 5 6 7 8 9 10	

	Not at all *satisfied*	*Very* *satisfied*

3. In general, how satisfied are you
with the intimacy you share with
your partner in this marriage?   1 2 3 4 5 6 7 8 9 10

4. In general, how satisfied are you
with how you and your spouse
communicate in your marriage?   1 2 3 4 5 6 7 8 9 10

5. In general, how satisfied are you
with how you and your spouse
express your love and affection for
each other?   1 2 3 4 5 6 7 8 9 10

6. In general, how satisfied are you in
your sexual relationship with your
spouse?   1 2 3 4 5 6 7 8 9 10

7. In general, how satisfied are you
with the financial aspects of your
life with your spouse?   1 2 3 4 5 6 7 8 9 10

8. In general, how satisfied are you
with the division of labor in your
relationship with your spouse and
the role relationships that exist between you and your spouse at this
time in your marriage?   1 2 3 4 5 6 7 8 9 10

9. In general, how satisfied are you
with how your spouse relates to
your children and his/her relationship with them?   1 2 3 4 5 6 7 8 9 10

10. In general, how satisfied are you
with the way that your spouse
handles his/her household manage-
ment responsibilities?   1 2 3 4 5 6 7 8 9 10

	Not at all satisfied	*Very satisfied*

11. In general, how satisfied are you with your relationship with your in-laws and your parents, relatives, etc., and their effect on your marriage and family life?   1 2 3 4 5 6 7 8 9 10

12. In general, how satisfied are you with your spouse's friends and your friends as a couple and their effect upon your marriage and family life? 1 2 3 4 5 6 7 8 9 10

13. In general, how satisfied are you with your spouse's work, job, profession, etc., and its impact upon your marriage and family life?   1 2 3 4 5 6 7 8 9 10

14. In general, how satisfied are you with your own work, job, profession, etc., and its impact upon your marriage and family life?   1 2 3 4 5 6 7 8 9 10

15. In general, how satisfied are you with how you and your spouse spend your leisure time together as a couple?   1 2 3 4 5 6 7 8 9 10

16. In general, how satisfied are you with your spouse's personal habits, appearance, behavior in public, etc.?   1 2 3 4 5 6 7 8 9 10

17. In general, how satisfied are you with the religious dimension of your life as a couple/family?   1 2 3 4 5 6 7 8 9 10

18. In general, how satisfied are you with the way you and your spouse deal with differences of opinion?   1 2 3 4 5 6 7 8 9 10

	Not at all *satisfied*	*Very* *satisfied*

19. In general, how satisfied are you with the way you and your spouse solve problems as a couple?   1 2 3 4 5 6 7 8 9 10

20. In general, how satisfied are you with how you and your spouse resolve conflicts as a couple?   1 2 3 4 5 6 7 8 9 10

21. To what extent are you satisfied with the degree to which your spouse has met your expectations for him/her and your marriage, up to this time in your relationship?   1 2 3 4 5 6 7 8 9 10

If any of the following issues constitute a current source of conflict in your relationship with your spouse, rate the degree of severity of the conflict for all that apply.

PART II

	Not at all *severe*	*Very* *severe*

1. Power struggle   1 2 3 4 5 6 7 8 9 10

2. Conflicts over values   1 2 3 4 5 6 7 8 9 10

3. Extramarital relationships   1 2 3 4 5 6 7 8 9 10

4. Spouse's personal problems   1 2 3 4 5 6 7 8 9 10

5. My personal problems   1 2 3 4 5 6 7 8 9 10

6. Conflicts over conventionality   1 2 3 4 5 6 7 8 9 10

7. Conflicts over intimacy   1 2 3 4 5 6 7 8 9 10

8. Spouse's jealousy   1 2 3 4 5 6 7 8 9 10

9. My jealousy of my spouse   1 2 3 4 5 6 7 8 9 10

	Not at all severe									Very severe
10. Problems with previous spouses	1	2	3	4	5	6	7	8	9	10
11. Problems with stepchildren	1	2	3	4	5	6	7	8	9	10
12. Personal illnesses	1	2	3	4	5	6	7	8	9	10
13. Spouse's illnesses	1	2	3	4	5	6	7	8	9	10
14. Personal physical handicaps	1	2	3	4	5	6	7	8	9	10
15. Spouse's physical handicaps	1	2	3	4	5	6	7	8	9	10
16. Spouse's alcoholism, addiction, etc.	1	2	3	4	5	6	7	8	9	10
17. Personal alcoholism, addiction, etc.	1	2	3	4	5	6	7	8	9	10
18. Verbal abuse by spouse	1	2	3	4	5	6	7	8	9	10
19. Physical abuse by spouse	1	2	3	4	5	6	7	8	9	10
20. Sexual abuse by spouse	1	2	3	4	5	6	7	8	9	10
21. Psychological abuse by spouse	1	2	3	4	5	6	7	8	9	10
22. Spouse is survivor of physical, sexual abuse, or incest	1	2	3	4	5	6	7	8	9	10
23. Self as survivor of physical, sexual abuse, or incest	1	2	3	4	5	6	7	8	9	10
24. Incest (past or present) in current family system	1	2	3	4	5	6	7	8	9	10
25. Other issues not listed: _____	1	2	3	4	5	6	7	8	9	10
26. How committed are you to your spouse?	1	2	3	4	5	6	7	8	9	10
27. How committed are you to your marriage?	1	2	3	4	5	6	7	8	9	10
28. How willing are you to make changes in your personal behavior in order to improve your marriage?	1	2	3	4	5	6	7	8	9	10

	Not at all *severe*	Very *severe*

29. How willing are you to divorce your spouse if he/she does not change his/her behavior in order to improve the marriage?   1 2 3 4 5 6 7 8 9 10

30. How willing are you to participate, with your spouse, in marital counseling in order to improve your marriage and resolve major conflicts?   1 2 3 4 5 6 7 8 9 10

4

The Assessment Interview: The Case of Mr. and Mrs. M.

In this chapter, some detailed examples for conducting assessment interviews within a managed mental health care practice are presented for the reader's review. The reader should pay particular attention to the following issues.

1. How the therapist helps clients quickly identify and focus on discrete problems or specific issues at the very outset of the therapeutic process.
2. How the therapist formulates a tentative diagnosis and how this formulation leads to the selection of particular individually focused assessment instruments.
3. How individually focused diagnostic instruments are introduced to the client and how any questions about diagnostic aids and assessment instruments are dealt with by the therapist.
4. How the therapist introduces the notion of collateral contacts to the client once he/she has approval to conduct collateral sessions.
5. How the therapist introduces marital assessment procedures into the therapeutic process.
6. How the results from individual and marital assessments are shared with couples and how assessment findings are used to help couples identify specific issues that are causing them concern.

7. How the therapist helps couples set realistic goals that can be achieved in the number of collateral contacts available to them.

The reader will note that in-depth descriptions of treatments and an analysis of intervention strategies are not the subject of this chapter. The author's goal is to demonstrate how concise and pragmatic assessments can be completed in a relatively short time and with a limited number of pretreatment diagnostic collateral contacts. It is assumed that the majority of the clinicians who read this volume are experienced practitioners who are already skilled in short-term and brief psychotherapies, but have limited experience conducting behavioral assessments with individuals and couples. Therefore, behavioral assessments are presented in some detail. Similarly, it is also assumed that the reader has limited experience using standardized individually focused diagnostic aids and relationship-specific measures in working with couples. Therefore, some discussion is presented of how these aids and instruments can be used to formulate realistic treatment goals, monitor the clinical process, and evaluate treatment outcome.

CASE EXAMPLE: MR. AND MRS. M.

Session I

Mr. M.:   Good afternoon, Dr. B. Thank you for seeing me on such short notice.

Therapist: You're welcome. Please have a seat on the sofa and tell me, as best you can, what prompted you to call for an appointment.

Mr. M.:   Well, I haven't been feeling myself lately. You know, I'm just out of sorts.

Therapist: When you say "out of sorts," what precisely do you mean?

Mr. M.:   I have little energy and I haven't been sleeping well.

Therapist:	How has your sleeping been affected?
Mr. M.:	I have been waking up during the night and having difficulty getting back to sleep.
Therapist:	Do you feel rested in the mornings?
Mr. M.:	Not usually. I feel sort of sluggish.
Therapist:	When you awaken during the night, what thoughts are you aware of? I mean, is there something on your mind that prevents you from having a good night's rest?
Mr. M.:	Well, there are several things. I am up for a promotion. I worry about that. My son and his wife just had their first child, and I know that they are having some financial difficulties since his wife stopped working. My wife and I have not been getting along well, and I need some major work done on my car, which will probably cost several hundred dollars.
Therapist:	I certainly can see how worrying about these issues can keep you awake at night. How have these concerns affected your performance at work?
Mr. M.:	My work has not really been affected. I try not to let these things get to me at my job.
Therapist:	Have these concerns affected other parts of your life? For example, your eating habits, sexual desires, leisure time, etc.?
Mr. M.:	I seem to be eating more and enjoying it less. I'm not much interested in sex, and I can't keep my mind on my golf game when I do feel like playing.
Therapist:	It seems to me that you are depressed. Would you say that this assessment is accurate?
Mr. M.:	Well, I do feel sad a lot of the time, and I worry that there are so many things I can't control or influence. Sometimes I wonder If I'll ever see my way clear.
Therapist:	How long have you felt this way? Is this depression recent or has it been with you for some time now?
Mr. M.:	I've been waking up at night for about the last three or four weeks. Usually, I don't dwell on things. I get

over stuff relatively easily. This is the first time I've felt this way, however, I just can't seem to shake it.

Therapist: What have you done to deal with these feelings? Have you seen a physician?

Mr. M.:   No.

Therapist: Have you taken any medication?

Mr. M.:   Only aspirin. Sometimes I get headaches when I think about these things for a long time.

Therapist: Have you ever used illegal drugs or alcohol to alleviate your depression?

Mr. M.:   No, I don't use drugs and drinking is against my religious beliefs.

Therapist: Let me see if I have this right. You say that you have been feeling out of sorts lately. You have a number of things on your mind that have been preventing you from getting a good night's sleep. You have felt depressed for about the last three or four weeks, but this is the first time you can remember not being able to pull yourself out of it.

Mr. M.:   Yeah, that's about it in a nutshell.

Therapist: Tell me, Mr. M., what made you decide to seek professional help now? How come you didn't call for an appointment, say, two or three weeks ago?

Mr. M.:   My wife suggested that I get some professional help. She said I was driving her nuts with my getting up in the middle of the night.

Therapist: Do you think that you would have sought professional help on your own? I mean, without your wife's urging?

Mr. M.:   You mean her nagging?

Therapist: Do you think you would have come in to see a therapist now if your wife did not "nag" you?

Mr. M.:   Probably not right now. Maybe if I still felt this way in another month or two. Who knows? Maybe never.

Therapist: In order to get a better picture of this problem, I would like you to answer a few simple questions. These questions are asked in the form of a simple

rating scale. There are seven questions. Would you be
willing to answer them now?

Mr. M.:   Fire away. Let's go!

Therapist: OK. On a scale of 1 to 10, 1 being least bothersome
or upsetting and 10 meaning the most troublesome
and upsetting, to what degree does your depression
bother you?

Mr. M.:   About a 7.

Therapist: About a 7?

Mr. M.:   Yes.

Therapist: How important, on a scale of 1 to 10—with 10 being
the most important end of the scale—is it for you that
your depression be reduced significantly?

Mr. M.:   About an 8 or 9.

Therapist: Again, from 1 to 10—with 10 being the most
important—how important is it for you that the
symptoms of depression, waking early, not feeling
rested, overeating, etc., be eliminated completely?

Mr. M.:   Again, about an 8 or 9, I'd say.

Therapist: Now, you said that your wife is also disturbed by
your waking up. Is she also concerned about your
depression?

Mr. M.:   Well, she does complain that I don't show much
interest in things the way I used to—especially in sex.

Therapist: Well, to what degree, on a scale of 1 to 10—with 10
being the most bothersome or upsetting—do you
think your problem upsets her?

Mr. M.:   I'd say about a 5 or 6.

Therapist: How important would you say reducing depression is
for her on a scale of 1 to 10—with 10 being extremely
important?

Mr. M.:   I don't know. Maybe if she thought I'd pay more
attention to her—maybe about a 5 or 6.

Therapist: Again, how important would you say that eliminating
your problem completely would be for your wife, on
a scale of 1 to 10?

Mr. M.:   Maybe 5 or 6.

Therapist:	Just one more rating scale question.
Mr. M.:	Oh, that's fine. I tend to see things in terms of degrees anyway.
Therapist:	OK. Again, on a scale of 1 to 10—with 10 being considered the most important or the most critical—to what degree would you say that maintaining your marriage is dependent on a significant reduction in your depression?
Mr. M.:	Not very. I don't think it is at all important or critical to my marriage. I don't think how I feel, you know, my mood, would cause my wife to leave me or me to leave her. It would just make life less tense for us, but I don't think my marriage depends on my being depressed or not.
Therapist:	You said, a little while ago, that in the past you have always been able to "shake it," your depression, that is. How often, over the past year, would you say that you got depressed?
Mr. M.:	This is the first time I ever remember feeling depressed. You know, sometimes I feel sad, like when a friend of mine dies or when my father had to have an operation, and we were all worried that he might not pull through, but those feelings didn't haunt me like now. Now, I go to bed with them and wake up with them.
Therapist:	Would it be accurate to say that these feelings of depression are not chronic, that is, that they have not been with you for years or for most of your life?
Mr. M.:	Yes, I'd agree with that, but I am worried that I won't be able to bounce back from them this time.
Therapist:	I can understand how this might be scary for you.
Mr. M.:	Well, a little. It stresses me out.
Therapist:	Well, let's try to get some idea about the scope and extent of these feelings. I'd like to ask you some more questions that will help us decide on a course of action. I'd also like you to complete two very short questionnaires between now and our next session.

The responses to these instruments will be very
useful in helping us develop a specific plan of action
to address the central issues that are concerning you.
Is that OK with you?

Mr. M.:   What kind of questionnaires are they?

Therapist: One is for assessing the degree of depression you
experience on a daily basis. The other measure is to
assess your daily stress levels.

Mr. M.:   How long do they take to answer?

Therapist: Each one will take only a few minutes of your time. I
suggest that you take a few minutes during the
evening, after supper perhaps, to fill them out.

Mr. M.:   OK. I can do that without a problem.

Therapist: Fine. Now let us turn to some additional questions.
Can you identify the places where you notice that
you become depressed?

Mr. M.:   It seems worse when I am at home.

Therapist: Have you noticed whether your feelings of depression
are more bothersome when you are at home alone
or when other people are at home with you?

Mr. M.:   I'm not sure. I really haven't kept track of my feelings
like that.

Therapist: OK. That is something we can explore in more detail
next time. If you can remember to notice if people
are present and who they are, or if you feel more
depressed when you are alone, that would be important
to know.

Mr. M.:   OK. I'll try to watch that during the week.

Therapist: What about your thoughts when you get depressed?
Have you been able to notice what you are thinking
or saying to yourself at these times?

Mr. M.:   Well, usually I'm going over things in my head, like
playing over and over again things that I'm worried
about. It could be anything–nothing in particular.

Therapist: I think it would also be helpful if you could pay
attention to what you are thinking and saying to
yourself at these times. You know, be aware of

	what you are thinking and saying that fuels your depression.
Mr. M.:	OK. I'll try.
Therapist:	Good. Now what about those feelings of stress? Do they occur in certain places?
Mr. M.:	Well, sometimes in the morning before I go to work. Sometimes driving to work. Sometimes at work in the morning. Sometimes at night.
Therapist:	Seems to happen at different times and places.
Mr. M.:	Yeah. Sometimes I feel stressed out when I wake up at night. You know, when I can't sleep.
Therapist:	So, sometimes in the morning at home, and sometimes on the way to work while you are driving?
Mr. M.:	Yeah.
Therapist:	Also in the morning at work?
Mr. M.:	Yes.
Therapist:	Ever happen in the afternoon at work?
Mr. M.:	Sometimes. It depends on what is going on at work.
Therapist:	Would you say that it occurs, the stress I mean, more in the morning at work or more in the afternoon?
Mr. M.:	Probably more in the morning.
Therapist:	And, of course, when you wake up at night.
Mr. M.:	Yes.
Therapist:	I am assuming that you and your wife sleep together in the same bed. You said that your waking up bothers her.
Mr. M.:	Most of the time. Sometimes she sleeps right through it.
Therapist:	Have you noticed any differences in your sleeping patterns when you sleep alone?
Mr. M.:	Well, my wife visited her brother about two weeks ago, and when she was gone, I had no trouble sleeping, but I did when she came back.
Therapist:	Well, Mr. M., I think we are off to a good start. If you can track your feelings of stress and depression during this week, we can start to formulate a treatment strategy next time. Here are the two questionnaires we talked about. One is the Beck Depression

Inventory. The Daily Stress Inventory is fairly specific. It will help you identify specific stressful situations and experiences. The Beck, on the other hand, is more global.

You may want to keep track of the relationship between stress and depression. For example, some people get stressed out first and later they get depressed. For others, it may be just the opposite, and for some people, both stress and depression appear to happen together—they feel both stressed out and depressed at the same time.

Mr. M.:   Well, Doc, do you think you can help me?

Therapist: I think that we can be successful if we isolate the stress-producing factors and the issues that are causing your depression. If we can work together and come up with a realistic treatment plan specifically designed to tackle these factors and issues, I think we can make some headway in the short period of time allotted to us.

Mr. M.:   Well, I hope we can. I'd certainly like to get rid of these feelings and get a decent night's sleep.

Therapist: I hope so, too.

Discussion

During the interim between the first and second session, the therapist consulted with the case manager to alert him to the possibility that collateral contacts with Mr. M.'s wife might be in order. Approval for including Mrs. M. in the treatment process was obtained before broaching the topic with Mr. M. at his next session.

Session 2

Mr. M. returned for his second interview with both inventories completed. The Beck Depression Inventory (Beck, 1978) scores for the preceding seven days were:

T   9 = normal
W   15 = mild
Th 14 = mild
F   17 = mild–moderate
Sa 22 = moderate–severe
Su 17 = mild–moderate
M   13 = mild

Stress scores as measured by the Daily Stress Inventory (Brantley, Cocke, Jones, & Goreczny, 1988; Brantley & Jones, 1989) all fell within normal limits, except for one score that rose one standard deviation above the mean. This score was recorded on the same day that Mr. M. received his highest (moderate–severe) scores on the Beck Depression Inventory (Beck, 1978). A content cluster analysis of the Daily Stress Inventory (Brantley & Jones, 1989) revealed that interpersonal problems and cognitive stressors were the two areas receiving the most emphasis by Mr. M. More specifically, items having to do with Mr. M.'s relationship with his wife were cited most frequently as stressors in both the interpersonal problems and cognitive clusters.

Responses to both questionnaires were discussed with Mr. M. in light of his own observations about events, circumstances, people, and cognitions that served as antecedent cues and reinforcers for his stress and depression. It became clear that feelings of both stress and depression began to increase as the weekend approached, and that theses feelings reached their zenith on Saturday–the day that Mr. M. and his wife were at home alone together.

Mr. M. was able to talk about his uneasiness with his wife and his uncertainty about their future happiness. He said that he spent "a lot of time" thinking about her and their finances and how their financial situation might affect their future. Prior to being asked to keep track of his thoughts by the therapist, Mr. M. had not been aware of just how concerned he had been about family finances. He had not made any connection between his worries about his possible promotion and his uneasiness around his wife. As he talked about these issues with the therapist, he began to realize that his concerns about his son also were part of this same financial theme.

It was at this point in the session that the therapist suggested that

Mrs. M. become involved in the therapeutic process. Mr. M. agreed and said he would discuss this possibility with his wife that evening. The therapist then proceeded to gather a history of the couple's relationship. When this had been concluded, the therapist gave Mr. M. a copy of the Pragmatic Marital Assessment Questionnaire (PMAQ) to complete and informed him that the PMAQ would be used to guide the marital counseling process and that Mrs. M. would also be asked to complete it if she decided to participate. The following day, Mrs. M. telephoned the therapist to schedule her initial interview. This first collateral contact with Mrs. M. is reproduced below.

First Collateral Interview with Mrs. M.

Therapist: Good morning, Mrs. M., please have a seat on the sofa and make yourself comfortable.

Mrs. M.: Thank you.

Therapist: As you know, I have had two interviews with your husband, and based on our discussions, I thought it would be helpful to involve you in our work for a little while. How do you feel about being involved?

Mrs. M.: I would like to do whatever I can to help him. He really is not himself lately, and I am worried about his moods, but each time I ask him about it, you know, if I ask him what's on his mind or if I say that he seems preoccupied or something, he says I'm nagging him. He has become so distant over the past few months.

Therapist: Sounds frustrating.

Mrs. M.: Well, I'm more worried than frustrated, but I must admit that sometimes I feel I'm up against a brick wall with him.

Therapist: Mrs. M., do you have any idea what might be preoccupying your husband? What he might be thinking about or worried about?

Mrs. M.: Well, I know he is up for this promotion, but he won't talk about it. I think he is afraid of getting his hopes up too high and then doesn't get it. I think he will really feel let down if this promotion doesn't come through. This will make the second time he has been passed over for promotion. If he doesn't get it this time, I think he'll consider himself a failure.

Therapist: That would be upsetting for both of you. It seems like there is a lot riding on this promotion. How is it affecting you?

Mrs. M.:   Well, mainly I worry about him. Sometimes I get sad and sometimes I get damn angry that he doesn't talk to me about what he is feeling and thinking, but mostly I worry about him. That's why I urged him, nagged him he says, to get some counseling.

Therapist: You are obviously concerned about your husband and his welfare. I can see you really care about him.

Mrs. M.:   I do.

Therapist: That's very clear to me.

Mrs. M.:   We always used to talk. It's not like he didn't communicate with me. That's what is so scary. He just stopped talking.

Therapist: I can see how this uncharacteristic behavior frightens you. Has this, this lack of communication on his part, ever happened before?

Mrs. M.:   Only once, when his father was sick and needed an operation. He just shut down until the operation was over and his father was out of the woods.

Therapist: Did you ever experience this breakdown in communication before your marriage?

Mrs. M.:   Not that I can remember.

Therapist: So you don't remember its happening while you were dating or engaged?

Mrs. M.:   No, I don't think so. Nothing stands out in my mind.

Therapist: How did you and Mr. M. meet?

Mrs. M.:   In an elevator (*laughs*).

Therapist: In an elevator?

Mrs. M: We worked in the same office building, and we would see each other almost every day. One day, Michael asked me if I'd like to have lunch with him, and I said yes. A week later he asked me out on a date. We began to date exclusively shortly after that.

Therapist: What attracted you to Michael?

Mrs. M.: He is a nice-looking man. He has a sensitive smile. He was, and still is, very polite and considerate. We are of the same religion and share similar values. He is respectful and a very hard worker. He is a good father to our sons.

Therapist: Sounds like quite a guy.

Mrs. M.: Yes, he is really a good husband, but the one thing that I noticed shortly after we got serious about our relationship is that he'd keep things to himself. Not that he hid anything from me or that he had anything to hide, but he just kept things that he probably should have shared with me to himself.

Therapist: How did that make you feel when you first became aware of Michael's keeping things to himself?

Mrs. M.: At first, I just thought it was that we didn't know each other too well and that as we grew closer, or after we married, he'd open up more. But that never seemed to happen. I guess I felt kind of disappointed. He is a lot like my father and my older brother that way. They keep things to themselves too.

Therapist: Strong, silent, and dependable.

Mrs. M.: I guess you could say that.

Therapist: How did your courtship with Michael progress? How did it move along?

Mrs. M.: We just continued to date exclusively. Neither one of us wanted to date anyone else. We just sort of kept going out, and after about six or seven months, he proposed to me. It was during the summer. We got married the following spring, in March.

Therapist: Looking back now, do you think you knew Michael well before you married him?

Mrs. M.: Yes, there have never been any big surprises. He is pretty much the same as he was then.

Therapist: Did you and Michael live together before you were married?

Mrs. M.:	No, I lived with my parents and Michael shared a house with a roommate.
Therapist:	Did you and Michael have any troubles adjusting to each other sexually?
Mrs. M.:	Well, I was a virgin when I met Michael. He had more sexual experience than I. We had sex together after our engagement, and it took me some time to relax and get into it, but by the time we married, we had developed our own style and rhythm. There was really no adjustment problem.
Therapist:	Has there ever been a problem in this area of your marriage?
Mrs. M.:	Not really. Not until now. I mean, his disinterest.
Therapist:	How do you feel about his disinterest?
Mrs. M.:	I think he's got a lot on his mind. I don't think it is anything I've done, but still I miss our sex life. I hope we can get it back on track.
Therapist:	I hope so too. Perhaps that is something we can focus on when we work as a couple.
Mrs. M.:	I hope so. It is not serious problem as it now stands, but it would be good to nip it in the bud, so to speak.
Therapist:	Yes, I think you are right about it not being too serious and probably being symptomatic of Michael's depression.
Mrs. M.:	Well, I'm glad that you noticed his depression. I had been wondering about whether he might be depressed. Do you think it is serious?
Therapist:	No, I don't see his depression as a major or chronic depression, but it is something that cannot be ignored.
Mrs. M.:	I know that, but I mean, do you think he requires some medicine? You know, Prozac, or something like that?
Therapist:	Well, I don't think medication is appropriate at this time.
Mrs. M.:	Well, I'm glad you don't think so, because I know some people who began taking tranquilizers years

ago and now they can't function without them. They get up, they take a pill. They have a hard day, they take another pill, and at night, they take another pill!

Therapist: I think I understand your concerns. At this time, talking about medication is premature.

Mrs. M.: OK.

Therapist: How have Michael's moods affected you?

Mrs. M.: I worry about him. Sometimes I get frustrated. Sometimes I get angry, and sometimes I get depressed myself.

Therapist: Would you mind completing some brief question-naires that would help me get a clearer understand-ing about how Michael's difficulties are affecting you and your marriage?

Mrs. M.: Are these the same ones you gave to Michael?

Therapist: Yes, they are.

Mrs. M.: I'll do anything to help. Sure, give them to me. Do you want me to do them here in your office today?

Therapist: It would be more helpful if you did these two—this one for depression and this one for stress—every day and returned them next week. This one, the PMAQ, you can just do one time. It gives us some sort of a baseline about the state of your marriage and what changes you would like to see take place.

Mrs. M.: Fine, I'll bring them all back next time.

Therapist: Good. Now I only have a few more questions I'd like to ask you before we conclude today's meeting.

Mrs. M.: Yes, go on.

Therapist: Let's get back to your decision to marry Michael. Were there any significant circumstances or life events that you think played an important part in your deciding to marry Michael, or deciding to marry him at the time you did?

Mrs. M.: Nothing comes to mind.

Therapist: What was going on in your life at the time?

Mrs. M.: Nothing. We were dating, having a good time. We

wanted to spend more time together. No, things were just going along fine. No hitches, no problems.

Therapist: How did your parents react to your decision to marry Michael?

Mrs. M.: Both Mom and Dad loved him. They were very pleased. They gave us a beautiful wedding and a honeymoon cruise. It was very nice all around. His parents are older than my parents. They took me in as their daughter. You know, Michael has two brothers and no sisters. They always wanted a daughter. I became that daughter. They are really nice folks.

Therapist: Well, it really sounds ideal. Sounds like a really smooth transition from single to married life. No hitches, no glitches—sounds pretty good.

Mrs. M.: Well, there was one glitch.

Therapist: One glitch? What was that?

Mrs. M.: My dad's money.

Therapist: Your dad's money?

Mrs. M.: Yeah (*sighs*). Dad did pretty well for himself, and when I got married, he gave me a big chunk of money. That made Michael a little uneasy. He is fiercely independent and he won't let me use any of that money if we are ever in a financially tight situation. I keep telling him that it is "our" money and not just "my money," but he won't hear of it. He says that it is our responsibility to deal with our own financial difficulties. I guess now that he is up for this promotion he sees it as an opportunity to prove that we still can handle all our financial obligations without using my "father's money," as he calls it.

Therapist: I see. It sounds like there is a streak of pride in Michael's character.

Mrs. M.: Maybe stubbornness is more accurate.

Therapist: Stubbornness is certainly one way of looking at it. Has there always been tension around money matters with you and Michael?

Mrs. M.: No, only when unexpected financial problems come up. You know, a big automobile repair bill or a medical bill that is not covered by our insurance, the kids' braces when they were little. You know, that kind of thing.

Therapist: We have all had our share of those, I'm afraid. I know that can be taxing.

Mrs. M.: Yes. Taxes also cause us some grief from time to time (*laughs*).

Therapist: (*Laughs*) That was not an intentional pun.

Mrs. M.: I know, but I just couldn't resist it (*Laughs*).

Therapist: So I guess the issue about money has been with you for some time. Sounds like it has been there since the beginning of your marriage.

Mrs. M.: Yeah, it is something we have learned to live with.

Therapist: Have you tried to get help with this problem in the past? Have you and Michael ever tackled this issue head on?

Mrs. M.: This is one of those areas where I can't budge him. He is like that brick wall I talked about. He won't talk to me, and he is too stubborn to get any professional help about his attitude.

Therapist: Well, now that you are both here, in counseling, perhaps we can all look at this problem together—see if we can all come up with some plan of action.

Mrs. M.: That would be great if we could do it, but I'm skeptical.

Therapist: I can appreciate your skepticism, but at least we can try.

Mrs. M.: Well, I hope so.

Therapist: Let's see if I have this right. You say that financial matters have been of some concern for you and Michael ever since early on in your marriage (*pause*).

Mrs. M.: Yes, that's right.

Therapist: But you and Michael have been unable to discuss them openly in any constructive way (*pause*).

Mrs. M.: Yes.

Therapist: And you have not sought any help with these matters—no help—professional or otherwise (*pause*).

Mrs. M.: That's correct.

Therapist: Tell me, how willing would you be to make changes in your own behavior as it relates to this problem—in order to come to some sort of successful resolution with Michael?

Mrs. M.:   Very willing. I'd do almost anything.

Therapist: Say on a scale of 1 to 10—with 10 meaning completely, 100 percent willingness to change—how would you rate your willingness to change your behavior as it relates to this problem?

Mrs. M.:   I'd say a 10—with no reservations.

Therapist: Well, it seems to me, based on my meetings with you and Michael, that both of you seem to be sincerely motivated to do something constructive, as a couple, about resolving your difficulties. I think there is good reason to be encouraged.

Mrs. M.:   Well, I hope you are right, Dr. B.

Therapist: The next time, when I meet with you and Michael together, I will have had a chance to review the instruments I gave you. Then we can have a more objective view of things.

Mrs. M.:   OK. I'll see you with Michael a week from Thursday at this same time. Is that right?

Therapist: Yes, that's the time Michael said would be best for him. Is that OK with you?

Mrs. M.:   Yes. I'll see you then.

Therapist: Good day.

Second Collateral Session: Mr. and Mrs. M. Together

Therapist: Good afternoon Mr. and Mrs. M. I received your completed questionnaires in the mail. Thank you for sending them so quickly. We can make use of them today.

Mrs. M.:   You're welcome. I try to get tasks like that done on time, and this means a lot to me.

Therapist: I know it does. Mr. M., thank you for taking the time to complete these forms two weeks in a row.

Mr. M.:	No problem.
Therapist:	Now that we are all here together, did you have any problem completing these questionnaires?
Mr. M.:	No.
Mrs. M.:	No, they were pretty straightforward—pretty easy to answer.
Therapist:	OK. I'd like to get right to a discussion of your responses.
Mr. M.:	OK.
Mrs. M.:	OK.
Therapist:	Mr. M. I notice that this past week your stress level scores all fell within normal limits and none of your scores on the Beck Depression Inventory reached the severe range. Actually, you only had one day, Saturday, where your score climbed to the moderate range. The rest of the week they were either normal or mild.
Mr. M.:	Yeah, I think this week was a little better for me.
Therapist:	Mrs. M. All of your scores on the Beck scale were in the normal range this past week. Only one score on the Daily Stress Inventory exceeded one standard deviation above the mean. This also occurred on Saturday.
Mrs. M.:	Yes, there was some stress for me on Saturday.
Therapist:	Can you tell me what took place, what happened on Saturday that caused you to be stressed, Mrs. M., and caused you to become depressed, Mr. M.?
Mr. M.:	We had a fight.
Therapist:	A fight?
Mrs. M.:	Well, not a fight—a disagreement.
Therapist:	What was your fight—your disagreement—about?
Mr. M.:	Well, Maureen suggested that we use some of her money to pay off some debt that we have accumulated over the past six months and...
Mrs. M.:	He wouldn't hear of it. You'd think I had suggested that we rob Fort Knox or something.
Therapist:	You sound hurt, Maureen, because Michael did not

want to accept your help. Michael, Maureen's offer got you upset. Her money seems to be a very sensitive issue in your marriage.

Mr. M.:   You got that right, Doc!

Therapist: When I reviewed your responses to the PMAQ, I was struck by how similar both of your responses were. You both indicated that intimacy, communication, and finances were areas of concern. Maureen, you also indicated some dissatisfaction with your sexual relationship with Michael. Michael, you also expressed some dissatisfaction with how you and Maureen solve problems as a couple.

Mrs. M.:   You know, I checked the sexual and intimacy questions, but they are really not the problem. These are just signs that Michael is worried and upset about things he can't control.

Therapist: Things he can't control. For instance?

Mrs. M.:   Like this money thing and our debt. That is really our problem. Do you agree with that, Michael?

Mr. M.:   Well, it is not the only problem, but it is the biggest problem. It has always been a problem.

Therapist: If you both agree that your financial situation is your chief concern at this time, would you be interested in making this issue—your finances and Maureen's money—the focus of our work?

Mrs. M.:   I'd certainly be glad to do that. If you can help us with this problem, I'd be eternally grateful. We have never been able to discuss these issues in a calm and rational manner.

Therapist: Michael, what are your thoughts and feelings about this?

Mr. M.:   Well, if you can help us do it without fighting, that would be novel.

Therapist: Then you would be willing to give it a try?

Mr. M.:   Yes.

Therapist: The case manager, Dr. S., has preapproved six collateral sessions. We have already used two of them, but I think that we can make some real progress in working through this issue in the four remaining sessions. I can teach you communication skills and a problem-solving/conflict-negotiation model that you can use to tackle this issue. Later, if and when other difficulties arise, you can use these skills to resolve them. How does that sound to you?

Mrs. M.: Sounds great.

Mr. M.: I'll give it a try for four more sessions. I guess it can't hurt, can it?

Therapist: The problem-solving/conflict-negotiation model I will teach you to use is a "no fault" model. There is no blaming or finger pointing. It is a "win/win" model. I have not known it to hurt anyone who uses it correctly. You and Maureen really seem to care about each other. I think you are good candidates and will be able to use this model in the appropriate way—the way it was intended to be used. No, I don't think it will hurt your marriage. It should improve it.

CONCLUSIONS

The case of Mr. and Mrs. M. represents a rather uncomplicated example of how individual and relationship measures can be used when collateral involvements are deemed appropriate. Mr. and Mrs. M. are ideal clients. They are not severely or chronically symptomatic, and their relationship cannot be considered one that is seriously distressed. Treatment goals can be formulated without much difficulty, and there appears to be sufficient motivation, trust, and caring between spouses to make a straightforward sociobehavioral skills-training approach to conflict resolution viable. Mr. and Mrs. M. are the type of clients that most clinicians would probably prefer, or at least enjoy, working with. They are ideally suited for managed care practice. In the following chapter, however, more complicated cases than the M. case are discussed. These probably represent the types of clinical challenges typically faced by many managed mental health care practitioners in their day-to-day work with capitated client beneficiaries.

5

Assessment in Crisis Situations: The Case of Ron and Sara

CASE EXAMPLE: RON AND SARA

On a Sunday evening at approximately 9 p.m., Sara called her managed mental health care company's 24-hour toll-free crisis hot line requesting a referral for emergency marriage counseling. At that time, she told the case manager on call that her husband had just returned home after being away for 48 hours. On the previous Friday, she and her husband had had a serious domestic argument that ended abruptly when he stormed out of their apartment. Now that they had had some time to cool down and think, they both thought that marriage counseling was in order. The case manager agreed and preapproved six collateral sessions. She made an appointment for the couple to see a therapist the next day, Monday.

Session I

Therapist: Good morning Ron. Good morning Sara. Please come in and make yourselves comfortable. Have a seat wherever you like.

Ron: Thank you.

Sara: I'll sit here in this chair.

Therapist: Wherever you feel comfortable. I spoke with Dr. T., and she told me that you folks were having some

72

	serious difficulties. It would be helpful if you would tell me, in your own words, what you see as the central problem in your marriage at this time. Who would like to begin?
Sara:	Ron, why don't you start? You're the son of a bitch who walked out...
Ron:	Don't talk about my mother that way. You got a mouth like a toilet. Just like your old man. I don't know why I put up with your crap. I should have left you long ago...
Therapist:	Excuse me. I'd like you both to stop for a second. I know that you both are pretty hurt and upset, but there are certain guidelines I ask couples to use when I work with them. You know, like ground rules for talking, listening, and resolving conflicts. The first one is not to interrupt your spouse when he or she is speaking. The second is not to attack, name call, accuse, blame, or threaten your spouse. There are several others that I will go over with you later, but for now, I'd like you to try to remember these two. Now, let's try again. Who would like to start?
Sara:	Well, we just can't agree on anything. Ron doesn't like my job. He doesn't like the hours I work, and he doesn't like the people I work with. He says they are a bunch of redneck lowlifes. He doesn't like my friends, and he hates my family. Well, not my whole family. Just my father and my Uncle Steve. I'm not attacking him. I'm just telling you like it is.
Therapist:	Ron, what are your thoughts and feelings about what Sara just said?
Ron:	She's right. I don't like her job, her friends, her father, and her uncle. She got that right.
Therapist:	Ron, from your perspective, what do you see as the major problem in your relationship with Sara?
Ron:	It's not only her work, her friends, and her family. It's a lot of other things.
Therapist:	Like what, for instance?

Ron: She doesn't take care of the house...
Sara: Well, I work hard all day. I need some help...
Therapist: Sara, let Ron complete his thoughts and feelings, and
            then you'll have a chance to tell your side of this
            story.
Sara: OK. I'll let him finish (*sighs*).
Ron: She doesn't take care of the house, and she doesn't
            cook very much. I do most of the cooking and
            grocery shopping. She is out two nights during the
            week at aerobics classes, and then she goes to her
            sister's house almost every week. It's like I hardly
            see her.
Therapist: Sounds like you really miss Sara.
Ron: Sure I miss her. I see my neighbors more that I see
            her.
Sara: Ron, don't you think that's an exaggeration?
Ron: Not very much!
Therapist: Sara, what is your view of this situation? What do
            you see as the central issue—the major problem?
Sara: He's too possessive. He thinks he's my father or my
            mother or some type of parent. He treats me like a
            child—like I have no common sense. I can take care
            of myself. I've been taking care of myself ever since I
            was 14.
Therapist: Ron's concern and caring for you make you feel
            closed in and confined sometimes.
Sara: Well, I don't know if he is caring or concerned, but it
            feels more like he's trying to control me.
Therapist: Ron's protection stifles you at times.
Sara: I don't need his protection. I said I can take care of
            myself.
Ron: So how come you get scared when you are at home
            alone at night sometimes? Why can't you sleep some
            nights when you think you heard a prowler outside
            the house? You want me there to protect you then
            all right!
Therapist: Well, it sounds like there are several areas in your
            marriage that require some attention. Would you be

	willing now to take a few minutes to complete a brief questionnaire that will enable us to zero in on some specific issues?
Ron:	Well, that's what we are here for, sure.
Sara:	This isn't one of those I.Q. tests, is it?
Therapist:	No, Sara. It is a questionnaire that has been developed to help therapists help couples identify areas of their marriage where major conflicts exist. It is not a personality test or an intelligence test. It is designed specifically for assessing relationship strengths and weaknesses.
Sara:	I took one of those MMPI tests at the psychology clinic at the university when I went for counseling there a few years ago, before I was married. The therapist there said I was hysterical, and I guess that I do get hysterical and fly off the handle sometimes.
Ron:	You got that right!
Therapist:	The questionnaire I'll give to you is not like that. It takes only a few minutes to complete and is not used for arriving at a psychiatric diagnosis.
Sara:	Oh, it really doesn't matter. I just wanted to know what type of test it was.
Therapist:	Ron, have you ever had any counseling?
Ron:	No, I don't like shrinks—pardon me, sir—I don't mean anything personal.
Therapist:	Nothing personal taken (*laughs*). Sara, would it be OK with you if I sent for your records—the ones they still have at the psychology clinic? They would be helpful, if you don't mind.
Sara:	Sure, but I don't remember my counselor's name. She was a graduate student. You know, an intern?
Therapist:	Yes, I know. Your records will be on file. If you would sign a written release, I'll send a letter with a copy of your release to the clinic director, and he'll take care of all the details.
Sara:	No problem.
Therapist:	OK. Here are the PMAQ forms. I'll step out of the office for a few minutes while you complete them.

After a few minutes, the therapist returned and reviewed each of their PMAQs. Both of their responses to the questionnaire indicated high levels of marital distress: Dissatisfaction permeated the relationship for both spouses in Part I. "Satisfaction with spouse" and "satisfaction with marriage" ratings for Ron were 4 and 3 respectively. For Sara., they were 2 and 2. In Part II, "power struggles," "conflicts over values," "spouse's personal problems," "conflicts over conventionality," "conflicts over intimacy," "my jealousy," and "verbal abuse" were cited as issues for Ron. Sara checked these same conflict issues and in addition "my personal problems" and "spouse's jealousy." Also in Part II, "commitment to spouse" and "commitment to marriage" were not given high priority by Sara (3 and 4 respectively). Ron, on the other hand, voiced a considerable amount of commitment in response to these two questions. "Commitment to spouse" was marked as 7 and "commitment to marriage" was 8. His willingness to make personal changes was also high (8). Sara's score on this question was lower (5), and she was much more willing to separate from her husband and to divorce him (10 and 8) than he was to separate from (6) and divorce (6) her.

The session resumed with the therapist's giving feedback to the couple about their responses on the PMAQ.

Therapist: Well, I've looked over your questionnaires, and they both indicate that there is a considerable amount of dissatisfaction and conflict in your marriage. You also have indicated that there are a number of areas where serious conflicts exist between you.

              Ron, you seem to be very committed to Sara and very committed to making this marriage work.

Ron: Yes, that's right. I've been married before and that divorce was something else. She took the kids and the house. With Sara, I thought I'd have a better chance to raise a family. I don't want to—I'm not ready to give that up just yet, but she makes me so mad sometimes that I just got to get away from her when she's like that.

Therapist: So you really want to make this one work.

Ron:	I'll do what I can. What's in reason, but I won't be a fool for a woman.
Therapist:	You won't give up your self-respect just to stay married.
Ron:	Yeah, self-respect is all a man's really got. You can't buy self-respect no matter how much money you got.
Therapist:	I understand. Sara, you don't seem to be as sure about Ron and your marriage. Would you say that is an accurate appraisal?
Sara:	Yes, but don't get me wrong. I really love Ron. He can be kind and generous when he wants to. He can also be a real pain in the butt, sometimes. He wants to be around me all the time. He smothers me. He's afraid that I'll be attracted to—you know—go out with other men, men who are more my age.
Therapist:	Yes, I noticed on the information forms you filled out that there is a seven-year age difference. Sara, you are 24, and Ron, you are 31.
Ron:	I'll be 32 next month. It's almost an eight-year difference.
Therapist:	Although you both seem to be pretty angry with each other, your coming to see a professional for counseling also tells me that you both sincerely care about each other and your relationship...
Ron:	That's true...
Sara:	Yes, we do, even though we fight like cats and dogs sometimes. Ron's always been real nice to me. Even when he's hoppin' mad, he's always been a gentleman. No rough stuff—you know—none of the macho shit.
Therapist:	He's never hit you or pushed you or anything like that?
Sara:	No, but I've thrown stuff at him in the past.
Therapist:	What kind of stuff?
Sara:	Pillows, a dish one time, and a bag of trash.
Therapist:	A bag of trash?
Sara:	Yeah, one night he said he didn't want to take out the

trash, so I picked up the trash and threw it at him. It was all tied up in a Hefty bag, you know, it didn't fall all over the floor or anything.

Therapist: I see, you have quite a temper.

Sara: I got it from my daddy. I have three older brothers and I learned early how to take care of myself.

Ron: But that temper gets you in trouble, Sara. You know it does. Not only with me, but on your jobs, and even in high school:

Sara: Yeah, sometimes it gets the best of me.

Therapist: Would you like to learn some ways to keep your temper under control? You know, learn some techniques that would help you get what you want without blowing up or getting into major confrontations?

Sara: That would be something new.

Therapist: Ron, what about you? Do you think you would like to learn how to work out your differences with Sara without having the kinds of blowups you've had in the past?

Ron: If it would help us get along, I'll give it a try.

Comments

This seriously conflicted couple presents a plethora of problems and difficulties that under ordinary fee-for-service conditions would require a considerable amount of time to address adequately. Under a managed care arrangement (e.g., six sessions), however, there is only enough time allotted to address one or two of the couple's major concerns. Research has consistently shown that active therapists who are able to step in and structure the couple or family's interactions early in the therapeutic process are more successful in helping spouses and families resolve the conflicts that bring them in for professional help (Gurman & Kniskern, 1981; Gurman, Kniskern, & Pinsof, 1986) than therapists who use more reflective and passive approaches to working with these systems. This active and structuring model is appropriate for work in managed mental health care settings. As can be seen in the above example, the therapist immediately steps in to structure the couple's communication.

He gives them some general guidelines for communicating in ways that make it possible for problem solving and conflict negotiation to take place (Bagarozzi, 1992b; Bagarozzi & Anderson, 1989).

Another important therapeutic strategy highlighted in this example is the therapist's use of *partialization.* He takes the initiative by suggesting that training in anger control would be very helpful for this couple. He knows that no constructive work can be done unless both spouses can learn to control their tempers. In all managed care work, the therapist is faced with having to make quick *but accurate* decisions since a considerable number of clients using managed mental health care services seek help during a time of crisis. In this example, the therapist *partials out* a major process issue (i.e., angry exchanges between the spouses) and zeros in on this as the first behavior to be modified. Such issues as jealousy, intimacy, power, roles, and tasks are judged as important, but the therapist knows that these can be dealt with more effectively in a nonthreatening atmosphere than in one that is characterized by anger and hostility.

Introducing Assessment

Let us return now to the interview with Ron and Sara to see how the therapist introduced assessment to this couple.

Therapist: Fine. It would be helpful for me to get some idea of how you both deal with your anger once you become aware of it. I would like you both to complete the State-Trait Anger Expression Inventory [Spielberger, 1991]. It is a very brief questionnaire—only 44 short-answer questions. It takes about three or four minutes to complete. How do you feel about filling out this short questionnaire?

Ron: OK.

Sara: Fine.

Therapist: There is another thing I'd like you to do. I'd like both of you to take these questionnaires and rate each question according to how angry you get when you think about each issue. Use a scale of 1 to 7–1 meaning not at all angry and 7 meaning very angry.

For example, let's take the first question: "In general, how satisfied are you with your marriage?" Let's say that you rated this question as a 3–down in the "not at all satisfied" range. How angry do you feel about this state of affairs? Are you a little angry, say 2 or 3, or are you to the point of being enraged–6 or 7? Do you get the idea?

Sara: You mean like question number 20? "In general, how satisfied are you with the way you and your spouse deal with differences of opinion?" I get pretty pissed off when he calls me dumb for not thinking his way about things.

Therapist: Well, on a scale of 1 to 7, how angry do you get when this happens?

Sara: About a 5 or 6. That really yanks my chain.

Ron: Like on this question–number 7. "How satisfied are you with the financial aspects of your life with your spouse?" I am very dissatisfied with that. I scored it a 9.

Therapist: Well, how angry do you feel about this issue?

Ron: I'd say about 6 or 7.

Therapist: Pretty hot under the collar about it.

Ron: You got that right!

Therapist: OK. Would you please use the next few minutes to do those anger ratings?

Ron: OK.

Sara: OK.

Therapist: I'll step out again while you complete this task.

Ron: OK.

Sara: OK.

Comments

In this case example, the volatility of the couple's relationship and the fragility of the couple bond, at this point, cannot be ignored. In order to work successfully with this couple, the therapist must intervene quickly to deescalate the negative spiral of reciprocal coercions and verbal punishments that characterize this couple's interaction patterns (Bagarozzi, 1980a, 1992b; Bagarozzi & Giddings, 1982, 1983; Rogers & Bagarozzi, 1983). It would be inappropriate to attempt to conduct individual diagnostic and history-gathering interviews with each spouse during this time of crisis. Stabilizing the couple's relationship is the first order of business. Similarly, since the couple's relationship is so volatile, the therapist asks them to complete the anger rating task in his office so that he can be available to help the couple deescalate any conflicts that might arise between them during the completion of this in-session task.

In-Session Exercise

Therapist: *(Therapist returns to the consultation room.)* I see you have completed the exercise quickly, How did you both feel about rating your anger?

Ron: Well, I didn't know how much anger I had about some of these things. I guess there is a lot of stuff stored up in me about Sara and the way she's done me.

Sara: I know I've been pretty angry with Ron. Maybe some of it is overdone—you know, if he tells me something, even if he's right, I'll do the opposite, just to show him he can't boss me around.

Ron: She's just like a little kid—stubborn—boy, is she stubborn!

Sara: Maybe I do act like a spoiled child sometimes.

Ron: Your daddy sure spoiled you, and that's a fact.

Therapist: If it's OK with the two of you, I'd like to spend the rest of the time we have in this session teaching you some communication techniques that will help you start to get a handle on your anger. They will help you get along better, in general, and they also form the basis—the foundation—for our work with anger

control and conflict negotiation. I said earlier that I
have some written guidelines for helping couples
communicate better. I'll give them to you now. Please
read them over carefully and, if you have any questions, please ask me. Then I can teach you these skills
and you can practice them at home between now
and our next session. I'll be your coach. You'll be the
team, and I'll be the coach who teaches you how to
communicate, negotiate conflicts, and solve your
problems. You know, communication is a skill—like
shooting a basket or riding a bicycle—anyone can
learn, and we get better with practice.

Ron: OK, Coach.

Sara: All right, what do we do now?

CONCLUSIONS

Flexibility, creativity, the ability to think on one's feet, and a good
sense of timing are therapist skills that are essential for successful
marital and family work. However, these abilities are especially
important and take on a different significance when one practices
in a managed mental health care setting. In this context, the therapist must be able to determine the degree to which a given couple
will be receptive to formal marital assessment and evaluation. The
managed care therapist must be sensitive to the possible negative
reactions that a poorly timed or an inappropriate assessment instrument, device, or procedure might arouse in a couple. The therapist
must consider whether a particular assessment instrument, device,
or procedure will strengthen each spouse's commitment to the treatment process or reduce the couple's desire to proceed with marital
counseling. For example, in instances where spouse abuse is a component of the presenting problem, individual diagnostic evaluations,
personal and marital histories (although more time-consuming),
coupled with behavioral observation of the couple's conflict negotiations and problem-solving attempts (Bagarozzi & Giddings, 1982,
1983), may be more important sources of data than the couple's
responses to a relationship-focused assessment instrument or inter-

view procedure designed to measure domestic violence, such as the Conflict Tactics Scale (Straus, 1979).

In this case example, the therapist understands that these spouses share a concrete and pragmatic view of the world and of their relationship together. Responses to "psychological tests" given by "shrinks" probably don't hold much value for them. Their here-and-now, solution-oriented approach to their marital problems lends itself to the short-term, problem-focused therapies that are the backbone of most managed mental health care programs.

6

Assessment of Developmental Transitions: The Case of Mr. and Mrs. Z.

CASE EXAMPLE: MR. AND MRS. Z.

Mr. and Mrs. Z. were married only a short time before difficulties in their relationship began to emerge. They had met while attending college, dated throughout their senior year, and married during the summer, after graduation. Both came from small towns where they had lived with their respective families until leaving home to attend a suburban university. Prior to graduation, Mr. and Mrs. Z. secured positions in a large urban center, where they took up residence after spending their honeymoon touring the southwestern part of the United States.

Both Mr. and Mrs. Z. were moderately depressed when they came in for their initial interview as a couple. Mr. Z.'s depression score on the Beck Depression Inventory was 17; his wife's score was 19. Both spouses agreed that they were having "adjustment problems." They had few close friends in the city, felt uncomfortable and out of place in an urban culture, and admitted to being nostalgic about small-town life and to missing cherished friends, siblings, parents, and extended family members.

The therapist spent the first part of the initial session taking a history of the couple's relationship. Both Mr. and Mrs. Z. said that they had nothing to hide from each other and each spouse felt very comfortable describing, in the presence of the other, his/her version of the couple's dating and courtship period. The accounts of their history, as a couple, were quite similar, and the therapist found no reason to question the veracity of their descriptions and recollections.

The second part of the interview was used to get each spouse's perception concerning the development and course of their presenting problems. Here again, both spouses spoke freely, candidly, and nondefensively about the sequences of events leading up to their joint decision to seek professional assistance.

At the conclusion of the couple's first interview, the therapist asked each spouse to complete the PMAQ, the Beck Depression Inventory (Beck, 1978), the Family Inventory of Life Events and Changes (McCubbin & Patterson, 1987), the Family Crisis Oriented Personal Evaluation Scales (McCubbin, Olson, & Larsen, 1987), and the Quality of Life Questionnaire (Olson & Barnes, 1982). These instruments were deemed appropriate by the therapist on the basis of the information gathered during the first interview.

Whenever pretreatment evaluations and assessments are a standard component of managed mental health care practice, time is a central consideration and cannot be overlooked. Therefore, it is important for the therapist not to misuse valuable in-session time by asking spouses and family members to complete questionnaires during the interviews. Although such a practice is sometimes appropriate when there is a crisis (such as in the case of Ron and Sara), in-session assessment should not become routine. If at all possible, the intake worker or the case manager responsible for making referrals to service providers should advise spouses and parents (when family therapy is deemed appropriate) that assessment is an integral part of the initial interview and that some assessments will be conducted during the first visit. The individual who is charged with making arrangements for the initial interview should explain the importance of pretreatment assessments, and prepare them beforehand.

In the above example, the therapist judged that three instruments, in addition to the Beck Depression Inventory (Beck, 1978) and the PMAQ, would be helpful in working with Mr. and Mrs. Z. A brief description of these three instruments is provided below for the reader.

Family Inventory of Life Events and Changes. This instrument is a 71-item questionnaire that makes use of a "yes/no" response format. It is designed to identify major stress events and changes in family life encountered during the preceding 12-month period. Each item is worded to reflect a change of sufficient magnitude to require some adjustment in the regular pattern of interaction life. The emphasis of this measure is on change. This change may be either positive or negative. When this instrument is used for an entire family system, five separate scores can be derived from respondents' answers: (1) family life event score, (2) family–couple life event score, (3) family–couple discrepancy score, (4) family readjustment score, and (5) family–couple readjustment score.

Standardized family weights have been assigned for each item for the two readjustment scores. These weights indicate the relative stressfulness of items, that is, the degree of social readjustment an average couple or family will make in its usual pattern of life as a result of experiencing each stressful family life event. Events are contained within nine general categories: (1) intrafamily strains, (2) marital strains, (3) pregnancy and childbearing strains, (4) financial and business strains, (5) work–family transitions and strains, (6) illness and family care strains, (7) losses, (8) transitions in and out, and (9) legal strains.

Family Crisis Oriented Personal Evaluation Scales (F-COPES). This is a 30-item scale that uses a five-point Likert-type format. It is designed to identify problem-solving and behavioral strategies utilized by spouses and family members in difficult or problem situations. Coping strategies are examined in terms of respondents' reliance both on sources available within the marital dyad/nuclear family and on sources external to the marital dyad/nuclear family. Items are behaviorally worded in terms of the strategies used. Items are grouped into three internal family-coping strategies and five external family-coping strategies.

Quality of Life Questionnaire. This is a 40-item scale. There are five possible response options, ranging from dissatisfied to extremely satisfied. Factor analysis produced 10 subscales: (1) financial well-being; (2) satisfaction with how one spends his/her time; (3) satisfaction with one's neighborhood, community, and educational facilities; (4) satisfaction with mass media; (5) satisfaction with one's home, physical space, and housing arrangements; (6) satisfaction with overall family life quality; (7) satisfaction with employment; (8) satisfaction with household responsibilities; (9) quality of health; and (10) satisfaction with one's religion, friends, and extended family relationships.

Assessment Findings

Satisfaction scores on the PMAQ for both Mr. and Mrs. Z. were high. Satisfaction with one's spouse was rated as 8 by both Mr. Z. and Mrs. Z. Satisfaction with the marriage was rated as 9 by Mr. Z. and 8 by Mrs. Z. Both spouses indicated low levels of satisfaction with how they relate to parents and in-laws, their leisure-time activities, religious involvements, and their friends as a couple. These items were echoed in both spouses' Quality of Life scores and their Family Inventory of Life Events and Changes responses. For the latter instrument, transitional issues were frequently cited, such as work-family transition strains; loss of friends, neighbors, and relatives due to geographical relocation; strains related to transitions "in and out" (i.e., unresolved separation–individuation issues from families of origin).

F-COPES scores revealed a similar pattern of stresses and concerns. However, perceiving herself as being cut off from her hometown church, which had served as a great source of strength, support, and hope for Mrs. Z., was dramatically underscored by her F-COPES responses.

Feedback Using Assessment Findings

Let us now turn to the couple's second session with their therapist to see how he used the information gathered earlier in the assessment process to help this couple.

Therapist: Good afternoon, folks. Please make yourselves
             comfortable.
Mr. Z.:   Thank you.
Mrs. Z.:   Thank you.
Therapist: I have scored and reviewed the assessment instru-
             ments that you filled out before you left last time, and
             I'd like to discuss the findings with you. Before I do
             that, however, I'd like to know if you have any
             feelings or questions about the questionnaires them-
             selves.
Mr. Z.:   Not really any questions, but they did make us think
             about a lot of things.
Therapist: What kind of things?
Mr. Z.:   Well, whether living in the city and leading a city
             life is the best life for us as a couple. Is living in a
             large city and raising a family here the sort of thing
             we really want to do? You know, those kinds of
             questions.
Mrs. Z.:   There really isn't a feeling of community where we
             live. We are a renting a small house now, but it is not
             located in a neighborhood where we plan to stay for
             a long time. We would not want to raise children
             there or send them to the public schools there. It's
             OK for newlyweds, but not for family life the way
             we'd like it to be.
Therapist: Yes, those are exactly the kinds of sentiments I felt
             when I reviewed your responses to the Quality of
             Life Questionnaire. You both indicated a consider-
             able amount of dissatisfaction on Factors III and XII.
             Factor III deals with neighborhood, community, and
             educational variables. Factor XII deals with religion,
             friends, and extended family relations issues. How-
             ever, your responses to the F-COPES questions were
             considerably different from each other's. Mrs. Z., in
             times of stress and crisis, you tend to look to social
             support systems, such as friends, relatives, parents,

neighbors, and your church, to help you get through difficulties. Mr. Z., on the other hand, you placed much more emphasis upon self-sufficiency as a couple and seeking professional help rather than turning to family, friends, relatives, and the church.

Mr. Z.: Well, Susie is too dependent on her family. I think we have to learn to stand on our own feet without too much help from others.

Mrs. Z.: Chuck is very adamant about being self-sufficient. I think he is threatened by having to turn to people for help, not professionals like doctors and psychologists, but family or friends, or our minister.

Therapist: What are your thoughts and feelings about what Susie just said, Chuck?

Mr. Z.: She's right. I really don't want to be complaining about how hard life is to my parents or my in-laws, and I certainly don't want Susie to complain to her parents.

Mrs. Z.: Chuck is very proud and independent, and that is really good. That's one of the reasons I married him, but I feel isolated.

Therapist: I know how important it is for young people to stand on their own two feet, and I think that you are both wise not to complain to your parents about the difficulties you are having during this transitional period. Building and solidifying a unified couple system is a family developmental task that is very important. However, building appropriate relationships with other significant systems, like the church, is also important for the growth and development of a couple system—and, later, a family system.

Mr. Z.: I know that, but we can't seem to agree on how to go about doing it so that both of us feel comfortable.

Mrs. Z.: I think that what Chuck says is at the heart of our problems.

Therapist: Well, sometimes in our efforts to be self-sufficient and independent, we may cut ourselves off from support systems and from appropriate types of help from parents, friends, the clergy, and other people who genuinely care about us and our welfare—people who really want to see us succeed—you know—they really want us to make it in life.

Mr. Z.:   You mean like some sort of overreaction?

Therapist: Yes, that is one way to characterize it.

Mrs. Z.:   Chuck overreacts sometimes, and that really upsets me.

Mr. Z.:   When do I overreact?

Mrs. Z.:   You know. How you look at me when I talk to my mother or my sisters when they call me or I call them. You get that look on your face—that annoyed look when you roll your eyes and wrinkle your nose.

Mr. Z.:   Oh, the look!

Mrs. Z.:   Yes, the look! The "give me a break" look! You get that same look on your face when my old friends call.

Therapist: Chuck, I sense that there is more to this issue than meets the eye. Is there something about Susie's relationship with her family that worries you or frightens you?

Mr. Z.:   Her sisters and her mother never seem to be satisfied with their husbands. They complain to Susie about what "the men" don't do. Susie has never done that to my knowledge.

Therapist: But that seems to be something that worries you. You're not sure that she won't find fault with you and complain to her mom and sisters about what you "don't do."

Mr. Z.:   Or even what I do do!

Mrs. Z.:   Chuck, you know I'd never do that to you. You know I am not like Helen or Carol, and I am very different from my mother.

Therapist: I wonder if some of this self-imposed isolation—the physical distance you put between your families and friends and you—was done to head off or protect you from such negative involvements with people back home?

Mr. Z.:   Well, I don't think it was conscious…

Mrs. Z.:   But we did talk about getting some distance from our families while we were dating, but I never meant to be cut off and isolated. That was not what I wanted.

Therapist: Looking over these assessment instruments you both completed, I wonder if it would be appropriate to start our clinical work together by helping you come to some agreement about how you would like to structure your relationships with other important systems in your environment—like your parents, siblings, in-laws, friends, and neighbors?

Mr. Z.:   I'm not sure I know what you mean. Can you explain?

Therapist: Sure. A very important part of building a viable couple/marital system is for both spouses to agree upon and erect an informational boundary or barrier around the couple/marital system. Like the membrane of an animal cell—a boundary that is not too rigid or too porous, but is permeable or semipermeable—so that exchange of valuable information is possible—allowing for appropriate interactions with other systems in the environment.

Mrs. Z.:   I think we have built a marital cell that doesn't let anyone or anything in or out. I think that is where my feelings of isolation come from. I feel Chuck stands at the gate monitoring what I say to people and what they say to me. Especially, when he gives me the look!

Mr. Z.:   Well, how do we go about building appropriate boundaries?

Therapist: Maybe we can start by talking about what type of information you think is appropriate for you to share with your parents about your marriage and your relationship with Susie.

CONCLUSIONS

There is no recommended procedure for introducing assessment findings to couples. Each couple is unique, and the therapist must take this uniqueness into account before giving couples such sensitive feedback, making interpretations about assessment findings, or suggesting a course of action.

In the preceding case, all assessment instruments pointed to the couple's difficulties being related to their struggles with marital systems formation, boundary erection, boundary maintenance, and information exchanges. Normalizing the difficulty that this couple was experiencing as a natural part of the marital/family developmental process is an important intervention that allows the couple to approach their clinical work as an educational experience—a task that they can learn to master with the help of an expert trained in family psychology and family life education.

Earlier in this volume, assessment and evaluation were characterized as ongoing processes of refinement. The marital instruments used by the therapist in his work with Mr. and Mrs. Z. were selected because they allowed him to canvass the broad area of *systems-in-interaction* that seemed appropriate for the couple's presenting difficulties. However, should the therapist suspect that the spouses are struggling with unresolved issues of separation/individuation from their respective families of origin, it would be appropriate to ask the couple to undergo further assessment with instruments designed to investigate these phenomena, such as the Family-of-Origin Scale (Hovestadt, Anderson, Piercy, Cochran, & Fine, 1985) and the Personal Authority in the Family System Questionnaire (Bray, Williamson, & Malone, 1984). When family-of-origin dynamics are determined to be central to a couple's problems, the therapeutic approach must become two-pronged. One focus would be the marital or nuclear family system; the other would be the spouses' families of origin. These issues will be dealt with in the next chapter.

7

Assessments in Context: Two Case Studies—Nuclear Family and Intergenerational Systems

In all family work, the therapist must be able to determine what level of systems functioning to address in order to deal effectively with the problems presented by clients. In addition, the therapist must make some determination about which family members ought to be involved directly in the treatment if therapy is to be successful. Intervention at the family systems level should not be taken to mean that all family members involved in the problem must be present in the therapist's office every session for treatment objectives to be realized. It does mean, however, that the roles that all significant others play in the problem's maintenance must be understood and taken into account when treatment goals are initially formulated and the strategies designed to achieve these goals are devised.

In this chapter, two different family systems problems are presented for study and review. Each problem requires a specific type of assessment procedure, and each problem requires a different intervention strategy to achieve successful resolution. Unlike marital therapy where only two individuals, the spouses, are seen together in the therapist's office, family therapy often requires the involvement of a greater number of people. Sometimes, persons who are not actually part of the nuclear or extended family system itself must also be included in clinical work if success is to be achieved.

Therapists working in managed mental health care practices must be able to use a variety of family interventive models in order to help the people with whom they work.

Since not all therapists who serve on provider panels can be expected to have been trained in a variety of family therapy approaches, it is the responsibility of the intake specialist or case manager, or whoever is charged with the duty of making referrals to therapists in the network, to match the family and its presenting problem with a therapist who has the requisite skills for dealing effectively and efficiently with that problem. Time and space restraints make it impossible to discuss, in any detail, therapist screening, credentialing and selection, administrative and organizational considerations, and the intake/case management procedures that need to be in place before appropriate client-family/therapist matching can occur. However, Bagarozzi and Anderson (1989) have identified seven potential therapist/family system mismatches that can render treatment ineffective.

1. Therapist × family system incompatibilities
2. Clinical method × family system incompatibilities
3. Therapist × clinical method × family system incompatibilities
4. Therapist × family–life-cycle stage incompatibilities
5. Clinical method × family–life-cycle stage incompatibilities
6. Therapist × clinical method × family–life-cycle stage incompatibilities
7. Therapist × clinical method × family–life-cycle stage × family system incompatibilities

The more such incompatibilities are reduced, the more likely therapy will be judged to have been successful by clients. In traditional clinical research, therapeutic effectiveness and success have been judged according to two interrelated criteria:

1. *Positive therapeutic outcome.* This criterion is the one that has been used traditionally by researchers to assess the impact of planned intervention. Essentially, the clinical researcher tries to determine whether therapy has indeed produced the desired outcome or outcomes initially agreed upon by

the therapist and client. Some of the most common examples are:

    a. the reduction of psychiatric symptoms
    b. decreases in negative affects and cognitions
    c. increases in positive affects and cognitions
    d. decreases or total elimination of undesirable behaviors
    e. the replacement of these behaviors by ones that are more functional, satisfying, or socially acceptable.

2. *Client's satisfaction with the therapist and the therapeutic process itself.* Traditionally, client satisfaction instruments have been used to assess this process (Barrett-Lennard, 1962; Anderson & Anderson, 1962). These instruments ask clients to evaluate the therapist's personal traits (empathy, positive regard, congruence, warmth, etc.) and the therapist's in-session behaviors (humanness, awkwardness, relevance, self-involvement, interest, etc.).

In managed mental health care practice, two additional criteria must be considered. These are:

1. *Client's satisfaction with the managed mental health care corporation.* Several issues must be evaluated to assess client satisfaction in this area. For example, satisfaction with:

    a. the types of programs available
    b. the type of coverage
    c. the number of sessions permitted
    d. inpatient/outpatient treatments
    e. the patient's experiences with managed mental health care personnel (e.g., intake interviewers, case managers, review specialist, psychiatric consultants)
    f. utilization review procedures
    g. the appeals process

2. *Financial costs to employers.* When thinking about financial costs, the employer using the services of a managed mental health care company cannot consider only the money spent for capitation each month (as his/her bottom-line figure) as a criterion. Several other factors must be taken into

account, such as the hidden value of defrayed costs associated with the reduction of lateness and absenteeism due to psychological factors (e.g., depression, anxiety, stress-related illnesses, psychosomatic conditions), substance abuse, and alcoholism. Similarly, managed mental health care corporations that allow coverage for collateral family contacts that make it possible (especially for single parents) to receive immediate professional assistance before crises develop at home, in school, or in the community may save the employer a considerable amount of money by averting a situation where the employee is required to take time off from work periodically or is forced to take a leave of absence to attend to critical family issues and difficulties.

Keeping this in mind, let us now proceed to the first case discussion in this chapter.

CASE EXAMPLE: MR. AND MRS. P.

Mr. and Mrs. P. had recently moved into this area from the West Coast. Mrs. P. was a businessperson and her husband was a real estate broker. Mrs. P. called for an appointment to discuss her anxiety, which had been worsening ever since she accepted a promotion and relocated to the South.

Therapist: Good evening Mrs. P.

Mrs. P.:   Good evening. I'm sorry I was late, but I had to get some last-minute paperwork done before I left. Again, I apologize for the lateness. I am usually on time.

Therapist: I understand. Paperwork can sometimes eat up a lot of time before you know it.

Mrs. P.:   Yes, this is true. Sometimes I have to stay late at the office to get caught up. That is part of the reason I'm here tonight.

Therapist: Oh, tell me about what you see as the problem.

Mrs. P.:   There are so many issues; I don't know where to begin.

Therapist: Let's start from the top. What issue is most pressing right now?

Mrs. P.:   My son Robert's behavior is having a negative effect on our home life, and that in turn has been causing me and my husband some difficulties at our jobs.

Therapist: What precisely is Robert doing that concerns you?

Mrs. P.:   He is having trouble at school, and some mornings he refuses to get up. Sometimes he gets up but dawdles so much that he misses the school bus and then either Henry or I have to drive him to school. Sometimes he refuses to go to school, and one of us has to physically take him. Recently, Robert began to mouth off with some of his teachers, and he was sent to the principal's office. The principal called me at work last week, because Robert had refused to leave his classroom after his teacher had told him to go to the principal's office. When the principal tried to get Robert to come to his office, Robert screamed at him and said that if he (the principal) or anyone else touched him, he would have them arrested for child abuse. The principal's call came when I was in the middle of a meeting with my boss and some out-of-town clients. I was so embarrassed, because I had to leave the meeting in order to get Robert out of the classroom. Now, the children in his class are beginning to call him names. Some of the bigger boys pick on him, and I think that he has upset his teacher so much that she looks the other way when children tease him.

Therapist: This is certainly a very upsetting situation for you and your husband, but especially for Robert. He must be angry and frightened, and I'm sure you and your husband are concerned about Robert's happiness, his welfare, and his future.

Mrs. P.:   Yes, we are, but we are also very angry with Robert's teachers. If they can't get him to mind them and they are the experts, what can we be expected to do? They said that they would like to have him tested.

They think he is hyperactive, and they want to put him in a Learning Disability class. You know, one of those classes for kids with very serious problems and profound learning disabilities. Robert is not learning disabled; he has an above-average I.Q. They also said that he might need Ritalin to calm him down. I said that that was out of the question! I won't have my child drugged and made into a zombie! That is unacceptable.

Therapist: I can see that this is very upsetting for you. You want to protect Robert—to help him—but the people at school only want him out of their hair, it seems...

Mrs. P.: Well, he is a handful, and there are 18 other kids in his class.

Therapist: You seem to be pretty understanding...

Mrs. P.: I am, to a degree, but this can't continue. It is really affecting my work. We moved here from California when I was promoted. I am the first woman in my company to ever hold this position, and now it seems like all the stereotypes about women in middle management are coming true for me.

Therapist: What types of stereotypes do you mean?

Mrs. P.: You know—"She can't take the pressure." "She can't decide between her work and her home life." "She's probably got PMS." "She wants to be treated like an equal, but she loses it when things don't go her way or when she is criticized." You know, that kind of stuff.

Therapist: I guess you feel like you are under a microscope at work—like folks are waiting for you to screw up.

Mrs. P.: Yes, and now this problem with Robert can really cause me some serious professional trouble.

Therapist: It sounds as if resolving Robert's school problems, or at least reducing them to a significant degree, would put you under less pressure at work. Is that so?

Mrs. P.: Yes, I think so, probably.

Therapist: In cases like yours, I usually work with the parents and child together, in conjunction with the child's teachers and principal. Does this sound like something that you and your husband would be open to trying?

Mrs. P.:   Yes, I know that Henry and I want to try working with you and the school, but Robert may be a bit of a problem. He is a strong-willed child. He may not even want to come here to meet you or to talk with you. He is an only child, you know, and he has always had a say in family matters.

Therapist: That's interesting. Are you or your husband only children also?

Mrs. P.:   No, I have two younger brothers, and Henry comes from a family of five. He is the youngest.

Therapist: Well, I am an only child. Growing up as an only child has its advantages, and it also has some drawbacks. When preparing Robert for our initial meeting as a family, you might mention that I, too, am an only child, and that we might share some things in common. However, as the parents in this family, you have the job of getting Robert in here so that we can all begin to work as a team—in a family teamwork effort to help Robert, you, and your husband enjoy a more peaceful and satisfying life.

Mrs. P.:   I understand.

Comments

In the example under discussion, assessment should take two different forms. For Mrs. P., a self-report measure of her anxiety, such as the Anxiety Scale Questionnaire (Krug, Scheier, & Cattell, 1976), would be an appropriate brief instrument to use. For Robert, a family interview plus behavioral observation of Robert at home and in school would be ideal. In order to carry out the latter two procedures, parent training in data collection, contingency management, and so on is required, and the therapist must be able to involve key school personnel in the data collection/treatment process if therapy is to be successful.

Carrying out such a treatment plan under the constraints of a managed care practice requires ingenuity and creativity on the part of the therapist. Approval for collateral contacts with Mr. P., Robert, and appropriate school personnel must be obtained before any direct intervention can be undertaken. If this is done properly and if all goes according to plan, no more than four collateral contacts should be necessary.

The time remaining in Mrs. P.'s initial interview (after the decision to involve her husband and her son in the therapy was reached) was used to help Mrs. P. discuss her feelings, concerns, fears, and hopes about her new position and her aspirations. Let us now turn to the second interview, the first collateral session, with Mrs. P., Mr. P., and Robert.

Therapist:	Good afternoon, folks. Come in and have a seat.
Mrs. P.:	Dr. B., this is my husband, Henry.
Therapist:	Nice to meet you, sir.
Mr. P.:	Nice to meet you too. My wife tells me that she has become more hopeful after her first meeting with you last week.
Therapist:	That's good to know. We can do a lot of work with just a little hope.
Mrs. P.:	Dr. B., this is Robert.
Therapist:	Hi, Robert.
Robert:	Hi, are you a shrink?
Therapist:	Some people might call me that, but I really don't shrink heads. I help people with their problems.
Robert:	Do you give kids medicine?
Therapist:	No, I don't prescribe medication. Why do you ask?
Robert:	Well, some of my teachers think I need it so I'll settle down in class.
Therapist:	Do you think you need medicine to settle down at school?

Robert:	No.
Therapist:	Tell me, Robert, do you play video games?
Robert:	Yes, I just got a new one for Christmas.
Mr. P.:	He is pretty good. He can play those games for hours and he gets pretty proficient in a short period of time.
Therapist:	Robert, do you have any trouble settling down when you play video games?
Robert:	No, I just sit down and play them.
Mrs. P.:	He doesn't seem to have any problems concentrating at home except when he has to do his homework. Robert's difficulties all seem to be related to his school and his schoolwork, and we can't figure out why.
Therapist:	Robert, what do you think about that?
Robert:	Nobody likes me at school. The kids pick on me and the teachers hate me!
Therapist:	Sounds like a real unhappy place to be—to spend so much of your time in a place where people pick on you or may even hate you.
Robert:	I miss my friends in San Diego. I don't like going to school here. I don't like living here.
Therapist:	You are sad and angry that you moved here.
Robert:	Yes, I hate it here.
Therapist:	It's a real bummer for a 10-year-old guy to move away from his buddies, isn't it?
Robert:	Yes, especially Sean.
Mrs. P.:	Sean was our next-door neighbor's son. He and Robert were inseparable. They went to school together, came home together, slept at each other's houses on the weekends, were in Scouts together. They were on the same soccer team, played video games, and even did homework together.
Robert:	He was just like my brother.
Therapist:	Yes, your mom told me you are an only child.
Robert:	You mean a lonely child.
Therapist:	Oh. I am an only child too…

Robert: I know, Mom told me.

Therapist: ...and I know what that lonely feeling was like for
               me. Tell me, what is it like for you?

Robert: Mom works hard all day and comes home tired. Dad
               works all day and comes home late. I sit at home
               after school and watch TV or play video games by
               myself. It is boring, boring, boring!

Therapist: Robert, how would you like things to be at home and
               in school?

Robert: I'd like the teachers to be nice to me and the kids not
               to pick on me so much.

Therapist: What about at home? How would you like things to
               be at home?

Robert: I'd like to do more things with Dad. I'd like to do
               more family things together.

Mrs. P.:   Robert, Dad helps you with your homework at night
               and so do I. That is something we do as a family,
               isn't it?

Robert: I guess.

Mr. P.:   Robert, we all go to church on Sundays together as a
               family, don't we?

Robert: I guess.

Therapist: Robert, I get a feeling that doing homework and
               going to church are not exactly what you had in
               mind. Is that accurate?

Robert: We don't do any fun stuff like we used to in San
               Diego. You know, the zoo, fishing—stuff like that. We
               don't even go to the movies anymore.

Mrs. P.:   Well, Robert, you have not been the easiest kid to be
               around lately. You complain when Dad and I try to
               do things with you. Your school work and your
               behavior at school have not been a pleasant experi-
               ence for either of us or for you. You give us a hard
               time almost every morning.

Robert: See, I knew you'd all gang up on me—just like at
               school. It is always my fault!

Mrs. P.:   You see, Doctor, this is the way he gets when we try

	to talk to him. The same thing happens at school when the teachers try to talk to him.
Therapist:	This is obviously a frustrating situation for all of you in this family. Can you tell me what you have all done, as a family, to get unstuck from this dilemma?
Mr. P.:	We don't believe in physical punishment. We try to reason with Robert, but he is very strong willed.
Mrs. P.:	We have taken away privileges and we have tried time-out—you know—sending him to his room, but that doesn't seem to work either.
Therapist:	I see. I suspect there are too many things in Robert's room to play with or entertain himself with for it to be used as a time-out room.
Mr. P.:	We have even tried to offer Robert rewards, but that only works for a short time. You know, we promise him if he gets up on time or goes to school without a fuss that we will buy him a video game. He shapes up for a while, but after he gets his reward, he reverts to his old stubborn self again.

Comments

At this juncture in the interview, the therapist must decide which course of action to pursue. There are two possible alternatives: (1) he can assume the role of parent educator and trainer, or (2) he can become a facilitator who helps all family members negotiate contingency contracts that will produce lasting structural and process changes in the family system itself (Bagarozzi, 1983c).

If the therapist decides to become a parent educator and trainer, he will have to teach Mr. and Mrs. P. how to observe their son's behavior at home, how to make objective and accurate recordings of his problematic behavior, how to identify positive reinforcers that they can use as incentives, and how to identify and use negative sanctions appropriately. If, on the other hand, the therapist decides to act as a facilitator in the family, he must then take the responsibility for conducting family interviews in ways that make successful in-session negotiations possible.

In managed mental health care work, the therapist must consider not only the issue of appropriateness of intervention, he/she must also consider the time required (in terms of number of sessions) to implement and successfully complete each treatment.

In addition to the decision concerning what type of treatment is deemed appropriate for this family, the therapist must also address the equally important issue of Robert's behavior at school. Since most managed mental health care organizations will not reimburse therapists for on-site school consultations and classroom observations, reliable and valid context-specific behavioral assessments of a child are difficult to obtain. The best that one can hope to receive from a teacher is a brief note or daily verbal report of the child's in-class behavior.

In order to get the school's cooperation, the therapist must be able to foster a cooperative working alliance between the child's parents and key personnel. In such cases, the therapist acts as a mediator between and among various interacting systems. Telephone consultations and conference calls that include both parents, the child, the teachers, and the principal must be coordinated by the therapist so that a unified effort to help the child can be mobilized.

Let us return to the interview with Robert and his parents to see what course of action the therapist chooses.

Therapist: Robert, I'd really like to help you get along better with your parents, and I'd really like you to have a more enjoyable and successful school experience. Is that something that you would like also?

Robert: I guess.

Therapist: Mr. and Mrs. P., I'd like to propose that we all work together as a team to accomplish two goals. One would be to develop more harmony and peace at home. The other would be to help Robert get along better at school. The goals are related. I think they go hand-in-hand.

Mr. P.: Well, I think the first thing we should concentrate on is Robert's school problems.

Mrs. P.:   I agree, the school is the worst problem. We have to do something to prevent Robert's behavior in school from disrupting our work.

Therapist: Robert, what is your teacher's name?

Robert: Which one?

Therapist: The one that you have been having some trouble with these past few weeks?

Robert: She's Ms. Colby.

Therapist: Ms. Colby?

Robert: Yes.

Therapist: And the principal. What's the principal's name?

Robert: Mr. Longstreet.

Therapist: Mr. Longstreet. That is an easy name to remember. Mr. Longstreet and Ms. Colby. Tell me, Robert, have you made any new friends at school?

Robert: Yes, Stephen and Peter, but they are in other classes. I don't get a chance to see them very much.

Mrs. P.:   They ride the school bus in together and come home together.

Therapist: Do they live within walking distance of your home?

Robert: It is too far to walk, but I can ride my bike over to Stephen's house, but my mother won't let me.

Mrs. P.:   He has to cross two very big intersections where there is a lot of traffic, and I'm afraid for his safety.

Robert: Well, all the other kids' parents let them ride their bikes across those streets. I'm the only kid who can't go. That's why some of the kids at school tease me and call me Baby Farts.

Therapist: Baby Farts?

Robert: Yes, Baby Farts and Whiney Butt!

Therapist: Baby Farts and Whiney Butt. I don't think I'd like to have those nicknames either.

Therapist: Mr. and Mrs. P., do you think that if Robert can get to school on time and leave your home in the morning without a fuss, he might be able to ride his bike to Stephen's house a few times a week?

Robert: It is not really Stephen's house; it is the city park.
               That's where Stephen and some of the other kids
               meet. You know, play ball, ride our bikes, stuff like
               that.
Therapist: Oh, I see. That is where you all can hang out.
Robert: Right.
Mr. P.:   Well, I don't see what that has to do with school
               problems.
Therapist: You're right. That will only handle one end of the
               equation—the home end. The school end of the
               equation is our next task. Would you give me written
               permission to talk with Ms. Colby and Mr. Longstreet
               about Robert?
Mr. P.:   Yes, of course. Anything to get this problem resolved.
Therapist: Thank you. Would you also be willing to discuss
               some sort of contracting arrangement with Mr.
               Longstreet and Ms. Colby so that they can help
               Robert settle down and enjoy learning at school?
Mr. P.:   Certainly.
Therapist: Robert, we will really need your help in this matter. If
               all goes well, the problem you have been having will
               be a thing of the past in a short time. I'd like you to
               think of what kind of relationship you would like to
               have with Ms. Colby and let's work together to see if
               we can help you have that relationship with her.
Robert: She doesn't like me. It will never work.
Therapist: Well, I will try to set up a meeting with Ms. Colby
               and Mr. Longstreet where we can all figure out a way
               to get things back on track. You, Mom, Dad, and I
               will all be there too. We won't leave you out. You'll
               be part of the planning—right from the start.
Robert: I don't think it will help.
Mr. P.:   Well Robert, I would like you to try it.
Mrs. P.:   Robert, I think this is a very good idea. You'll see, it
               is the best thing to do—to have all the key people
               involved—that really is the best way to do it.

Conclusions

From the above excerpt, it can be seen that the therapist opted for the less formal family contracting approach instead of the more structured, parent-dominated, behavior-modification alternative. The reader will immediately notice that no pretreatment baseline data are collected in this informal approach. A simple "if-then" contingency arrangement is worked out among the family members.

When contracts of this sort are negotiated in families, the terms of the agreement should be written down and posted in a prominent place in the home so that they can serve as stimulus cues. They also help avoid any misunderstanding among the participants.

A similar procedure can then be attempted with school personnel for charges in the child's classroom behavior, if teachers and school officials are willing to work with the family and the therapist. Contracts made with teachers for classroom compliance should include in-school token reinforcers that the child can earn and bring home to the parents, who then provide the child with the agreed-upon earned privilege.

When behavioral and contingency contracts of this sort are used in situations where no baseline data have been collected to serve as pretreatment measures of problematic behavior, reports from teachers, parents, and any other significant participants should be considered legitimate measures of therapeutic effectiveness by managed mental health care companies.

CASE EXAMPLE: THE X FAMILY

First Session

Therapist: Good afternoon, Mrs. X. Please come in and have a seat.

Mrs. X.:   Thank you, Doctor. Well, I know that you have talked with Ms. Conroy, the intake person, and that she has told you about my problem. Do you think that you can help us?

Therapist: Yes, I have spoken with Mrs. Conroy, and she said you are having some difficulties at home that are affecting your work, but I don't know much more than that. It would be helpful if you would describe the problem in your own words first, and then we can try to come up with a concrete plan to resolve whatever it is that is causing you distress.

Mrs. X.:   I guess that there are two problems—well, actually three problems.

Therapist: OK. Why don't you talk about them in their order of importance. Which is the most disturbing and upsetting?

Mrs. X.:   That is hard to say. They are all sort of connected. I'm not sure that you can really separate the three of them.

Therapist: They all seem to run together. I guess that it must be confusing and a lot to handle at one time.

Mrs. X.:   Sometimes they all come crashing down at once, and I feel like I can't breathe and that I'll never get it all together.

Therapist: Sort of overwhelming.

Mrs. X.:   Yes, very. Sometimes I get so nervous I feel like jumping out of my skin. Sometimes I can't get to sleep at night because I have so many thoughts running through my head.

Therapist: How long have these feelings of anxiety been with you?

Mrs. X.:   Well, I've always been hyper. Even as a child, I could not sit still. My mother always fussed at me because I was so active. It has gotten better as I got older, but these last few weeks, I've really been going 90 miles a minute.

Therapist: What has been happening these past few weeks?

Mrs. X.:   I have been dreading my mother's visit. My mother is a real critical person. She criticizes me. She criticizes my housekeeping. She criticizes my job. She doesn't like my second husband at all, and she thinks I'm too strict with my children. I don't know why I let her upset me so much. I see her only once or twice a year, but before each visit, I find myself getting very uptight.

Therapist: So you and your mother have had a lot of friction in your relationship?

Mrs. X.:   Friction! That's putting it mildly. We fought like cats and dogs when I was a teenager. After my father died, before she remarried, I ran away from home to get away from her nagging. I left home after high school and got married, the first time, when I was 20.

Therapist: Pretty stormy family life.

Mrs. X.:   After my divorce, she blamed me for all the problems Kenneth and I had. She said I drove him away. Kenneth was really a sweet person, a nice guy, but he could not stand up to my mother—that's why she liked him so much. She could run all over him like she ran over my dad and my stepdad, but she can't run over Clark.

Therapist: Clark, is he your husband?

Mrs. X.:   Yes, he won't put up with her crap. He tries not to interact with her very much. They both give each other a lot of room when they are together, but when she interferes with how we treat the children, Clark will tell her to mind her own business. Then I find myself caught in the middle.

Therapist: Between a rock and a hard place.

Mrs. X.:   Exactly! A real hard place. So, you see what I mean? There is the problem with Mom and that creates tension between me and Clark, and then there is the problem she causes with our children. Every time we visit my mother or she visits us, the kids play us off against each other. Mom spoils them and takes their side when we discipline them. After a visit, it takes several days before they settle down.

Therapist: How old are your children?

Mrs. X.:   Kenneth, Jr. is 11 and Paul will be 8 next month.

Therapist: Kenneth is from your first marriage, I gather?

Mrs. X.:   Yes, and that's another problem. My mother is always bringing up his father and what a wonderful man he is and how nice his second wife is and blah, blah, blah! That really doesn't help much.

Therapist: No. I'm sure it doesn't.

Mrs. X.:   Our kids are really nice kids, but when their grandmother is around, they can really push our patience.

Therapist: Is this the full scope of the problem or are there some other issues that we need to look at?

Mrs. X.:   No, that is pretty much it. Can you help me? My mother is coming into town in four weeks and I'd like to chill out before she gets here, and I blow the roof off everything.

Therapist: That is a pretty tall order. It would be wonderful if we could do something immediately to bring some peace, understanding, and mutual respect between you and your mother, but this feud has been going on for quite a while. Let's think about what is a realistic goal to set for this up and coming visit, then we can talk about some long-range goals and plans once this visit is over. We can also use this visit to collect some information, to make some observations. We can make this visit work to our advantage and use it as a learning experience—so we can plan a strategy for the next visit.

Mrs. X.:   OK. How do we start?

Comments

In this initial session, the client presented a number of complex and interrelated problems that do not readily lend themselves to quick and easy behavioral solutions. When several difficult issues of this type are identified by a client, it is probably not clinically wise to introduce a global assessment instrument, such as the PMAQ, since such a measure may serve only to identify additional problems that might increase the client's distress and compound his/her feelings of being overwhelmed.

These considerations are especially relevant in managed care work whenever clients have limited mental health coverage. Learning that one has additional and significant interpersonal problems that the client had not previously recognized (or had been denying) and knowing that there is insufficient mental health coverage to treat these problems adequately may only produce increased feelings of frustration, depression, anxiety, and helplessness. The best strategy is to help the client *partialize* and focus on those issues that can be treated successfully within the parameters of the coverage available.

At this point in treatment, assessment for Mrs. X. should take two forms: (1) evaluation of her anxiety through one of the individually focused instruments discussed earlier in this volume, and (2) intergenerational assessment.

Probably, the best measure available to assess the negative effects of unresolved intergenerational influences on one's current life and nuclear family is the Personal Authority in the Family Systems Questionnaire (Bray, Williamson, & Malone, 1984). Although the PAFS-Q has been shown to be reliable and valid (L'Abate & Bagarozzi, 1992), this 132-item instrument takes considerable time to complete (15–20 minutes). Eight factor-derived scales, however, offer important, clinically relevant information. The eight scales assess: (1) intergenerational intimidation, (2) intergenerational triangulation, (3) intergenerational fusion and individuation, (4) intergenerational intimacy, (5) personal authority via one's parents and one's spouse, (6) triangulation of children in one's own nuclear family, (7) intimacy with one's spouse, and (8) autonomy/individuation in relation to one's partner.

In addition to giving the therapist clinically useful information about the client's degree of enmeshment in his/her family of origin, the PAFS-Q also identifies strengths and weaknesses in the client's nuclear family system. The more solid the marital relationship and nuclear family system are found to be, the better the prognosis will be for a positive outcome for intergenerationally focused therapy.

In response to Mrs. X.'s question about where to begin, the therapist suggested that she might be able to identify specific treatment issues more accurately if she took some time to complete the PAFS-Q during the week and return it to him for scoring before her next interview. She agreed to do so. The therapist also suggested that their next session be a conjoint one that included her husband. He stressed the importance of having her husband as an ally throughout the process of intergenerational therapy, and she agreed that his support was important to her. Finally, near the end of the interview, the therapist asked Mrs. X. if she would complete the IPAT Anxiety Scale (Krug, Scheier, & Cattell, 1976) before she left his office. This measure would be used to make pretreatment/posttreatment assessment of change.

Let us now turn to the second interview, the first collateral marital session, to see how PAFS-Q information was used by the therapist to strengthen the marital bond and to formulate a viable treatment strategy.

Second Session

Therapist: Good evening, Mrs. X. Good evening, Mr. X. Thank you for agreeing to come. Your support and assistance are very important and valuable.

Mr. X.: Thank you for asking me to accompany Cathy.

Mrs. X.: Clark can be very helpful when it comes to my family—especially my mother.

Therapist: It is good to know that you are allies in this project. Perhaps, if we all play our cards right, you can develop a better relationship with your mother.

Mr. X.: I'm not so sure about that. She is one tough cookie.

Mrs. X.: At least we can try to call a truce.

Mr. X.: A truce would be nice. We'd have some peace and quiet at least.

Mrs. X.: That would be different. That would be nice.

Mrs. X.: Well, Doctor, what did my test tell you about my problem with my family?

Therapist: Several things become clear as I scored the
             questionnaire.
Mrs. X.:   What did you find out?
Therapist: The questionnaire you completed allows us to assess
             several aspects of your family of origin and your
             nuclear family—your relationship with Clark and your
             children. Your responses were very encouraging. For
             the two areas that focus on your nuclear family, your
             scores indicate that you and Clark have a very inti-
             mate relationship that does not interfere with your
             autonomy—your separateness and independence as
             individuals. This finding is certainly a desirable one.
Mrs. X.:   Yes, I think this is true. Even though I have not
             taken this test, I think I would agree with Cathy's
             perception.
Therapist: That is certainly helpful to know that you agree with
             Cathy's perceptions of intimacy in your marriage.
             The more spouses agree on critical factors such as
             love and intimacy, the more satisfying their marriages
             tend to be. You know, the more spouses see eye to
             eye on things, the smoother the relationship.
Mr. X.:   Cathy and I agree on most things—most things that
             count—I would say.
Therapist: What do you feel about your husband's statements?
Mrs. X.:   I agree. Our marriage is not a problem. We agree on
             most of the important things, but how to deal with
             my mother is a real sore point.
Therapist: I see. Dealing with your mother is a source of conflict
             for you?
Mr. X.:   Yes, most of the time.
Mrs. X.:   A lot of the time.
Therapist: I know that your children seem to get caught in the
             middle of your relationship with your mother, and it
             seems that they also get caught between the two of
             you—to some degree.
Mrs. X.:   Yes, you know, two children with different fathers can
             cause problems sometimes.

Therapist: Yes, that does happen more often than not.

Mrs. X.:   It seems to happen more when my mother is around, I think. Don't you agree, Clark?

Mr. X.:   Yes, definitely.

Therapist: Well, that is one area we can focus on in our work together.

Mrs. X.:   Good.

Mr. X.:   Excellent!

Therapist: The other areas where problems were identified by you, Cathy, had to do with the intimacy, or I should say the lack of intimacy, between you and your mother. It appears that, for some reason, you are also caught up in your parents' relationship somehow. Is that accurate?

Mrs. X.:   Well, not my parents' relationship, but caught between my mother and stepfather. Remember, my father died when I was 13.

Therapist: Yes, thank you for reminding me. You seem caught between your mother and your stepfather.

Mrs. X.:   Yes.

Therapist: Your responses show that—in spite of the difficulties you have with your mother and stepfather—you have been able to achieve a good deal of personal authority.

Mrs. X.:   What does that mean?

Therapist: You have been pretty successful in your ability to function autonomously from your mother, and you seem to have developed an age-appropriate, adult–child to adult–parent relationship with her and your stepfather, for the most part.

Mrs. X.:   Well, not all the time.

Therapist: Yes, I understand, but much of the time.

Mrs. X.:   Yes, especially when Clark is around. He can keep me cool.

Therapist: Another thing is that you don't seem to be intimidated by your mother. The Intergenerational

Intimidation score you received shows you to not feel intimidated either by your mother or your stepfather.

Mrs. X.: That's true. We have been at each other ever since I was a child. I'm not afraid of her. She just makes me mad!

Therapist: The bond that the two of you have developed as husband and wife is a very valuable one. We can use that teamwork bond to our advantage. Clark, would you be willing to work with Cathy—to be her partner—and with me so that a new and more satisfying relationship might be developed between Cathy and her mother?

Mr. X.: Yes, of course.

Therapist: Your input and support are critical.

Mr. X.: I know. I'll do what I can.

Conclusions

The information gathered through the use of the PAFS-Q can be very useful in managed care work in spite of the instrument's length, since it helps both the client and the therapist focus on specific intergenerational issues. The therapist's role is to help Mrs. X. translate these global issues into concrete behavioral objectives and desirable interpersonal (i.e., intergenerational) outcomes. Goal attainment can be facilitated, in many instances, through the use of various ancillary clinical services and techniques. In managed mental health care practice, the therapist must know the various community-sponsored programs and services that clients can use to augment and support the work they are doing with them.

It is especially important for managed mental health practitioners to be able to refer clients to community-based programs that are inexpensive, yet effective. For example, once an agreed-upon behavioral goal was formulated with Mrs. X. and her husband, the therapist suggested that she might consider attending a low-cost assertiveness training program being offered at a community clinic near her home. Assertiveness was seen, by her therapist, as a valuable skill that Mrs. X. could use in her intergenerational work with her mother.

Mrs. X.'s scores on the IPAT Anxiety scale were found to be high. This was not unexpected given her descriptions of herself as a child and adolescent. Therefore, the therapist also suggested that she might consider enrolling in a six-week stress and anxiety-reduction workshop that was being offered at a local hospital.

Another important consideration that should not be overlooked is the strategic spacing of therapy sessions by the managed mental health practitioner. In intergenerational work, within the context of managed mental health care practice, the therapist must work closely with the client (and his/her spouse) to devise homework assignments that are specifically tailored to help the client achieve concrete behavioral goals and interpersonal outcomes with several members of his/her family of origin. It may, however, require several training and practice sessions before the client learns and masters the interpersonal skills necessary to execute the agreed-upon intergenerational homework assignment successfully.

For example, in the case of Mrs. X., she and her therapist agreed upon a goal of trying to minimize her mother's success in attempting to triangulate her children and to coalign with them against Mrs. X. To accomplish this one specific goal, Mrs. X. was referred to the assertiveness training program where she learned non-aggressive and nonantagonistic ways to set limits with others—particularly with her mother. The therapist did not meet with Mrs. X. until she had participated in three assertiveness training sessions. During this time between sessions with her managed care therapist, Mrs. X. practiced responding assertively with her husband, who role-played the part of Mrs. X.'s mother. The managed care therapist checked in with Mrs. X. prior to and immediately following each training session to monitor her progress. Mrs. X. also gave her therapist written permission to consult with and share information about her progress with her assertiveness training instructor.

Two weeks elapsed between Mrs. X.'s second visit (i.e., her first collateral visit) and her third session with her therapist (i.e., her second cojoint session with her husband). The second collateral session was used to (a) help Mrs. X. practice her newly acquired assertiveness skills in preparation for her mother's arrival, (b) teach Mrs. X. how to make objective observations about her own success in implementing her recently developed skills, and (c) teach Mr. and Mrs. X. how to collect baseline data on other problematic behaviors exhibited by her mother.

Mrs. X.'s fourth and final session was a debriefing and outcome evaluation session that was held several days after Mrs. X.'s mother and stepfather departed. The therapist reviewed with Mrs. X. her mother's interactions with her and her children, her feelings about this visit, and her current relationship with her mother. The therapist then reviewed the observational data collected by Mrs. X. during the course of her mother's visit. She and the therapist were able to underscore several additional issues that would require attention before her next encounter with her mother. Before leaving the therapist's office, Mrs. X. again completed the IPAT Anxiety Scale. This served as a posttreatment evaluation of her anxiety level. Mrs. X. said that she would be in touch with the therapist to schedule some additional sessions before visiting her mother and stepfather during her summer vacation.

A month after terminating with Mrs. X., the therapist mailed her the IPAT Anxiety Scale and the PAFA-Q for completion in order to assess the degree to which therapeutic gains were being maintained.

8

Accountability in Managed Mental Health Care Practice

The issue of accountability in managed mental health care practice is complex and multifaceted. First and foremost, in this author's opinion, employers, managed mental health care entities, and service providers all owe their primary responsibility to the client beneficiaries they serve.

The employer who elects to offer mental health coverage to employees as part of the benefit package must also take the responsibility for making certain that he/she has selected the best possible mental health care service option available, given the company's overall budgetary constraints, its fiscal limitations, and the employees' ability to pay their share of the monthly premiums necessary to meet the cost of coverage. However, the employer's responsibility to employees does not stop there. It is this author's contention that any employer who contracts with a managed mental health care organization for services also has the responsibility to make sure that these services are evaluated periodically. Furthermore, all evaluations of the managed mental health care organization's performance initiated by the employer should be carried out independently of and in addition to any studies of outcome success and client satisfaction conducted by the managed mental health care entity itself.

EMPLOYER RESPONSIBILITIES

Employer assessments of managed mental health care service delivery should include inquiries into client beneficiaries' satisfaction with the comprehensiveness of their coverage. Issues having to do with exclusionary clauses and preexisting conditions should be addressed. The client beneficiaries' satisfaction with any conversion options available to them should be considered. Employees' satisfaction with the financial responsibilities they are required to shoulder (e.g., deductibles, copayments, premiums) should also be reviewed.

The next issue for the employer to investigate is the employees' satisfaction with the overall administrative functioning of the managed mental health care entity as it relates to them. Such factors as accessibility, helpfulness, knowledge, and courtesy on the part of managed mental health care staff and personnel responsible for answering questions about benefits, coverage, procedures, claims, processing, precertification, etc. should be a major consideration for the employer.

Similarly, employee satisfaction with the promptness and appropriateness of referrals to panel members made by intake personnel, case managers, review specialists, and the like must also be reviewed carefully by the employer. In situations in which no panel members have the requisite expertise to treat a client beneficiary's problem and in instances where the services needed by an employee are not covered under the company's contract, the employer must investigate whether the managed mental health care organization did fulfill its professional, ethical, and legal obligation to secure the appropriate care for the employee and whether the employee was satisfied with the managed mental health care corporation's handling of the matter. When precertification for hospitalization is required, especially in cases where there is a psychiatric emergency, the employer must look into how these procedures were handled by the managed care corporation and whether the employees who needed emergency services received appropriate attention, timely care, and adequate treatment.

Next, the employer has the responsibility of assessing the employees' satisfaction with the clinical/counseling process itself. Employee satisfaction with the following procedures should be carefully reviewed: (a) intake process, (b) diagnostic interviews, (c) psychiatric evaluations and consultations, (d) psychological testing procedures, (e) referral and assignment process, (f) confidentiality, and (g) continuity of care. Obviously, the employee's satisfaction with the therapist or therapists to whom he/she was referred is of paramount importance. In order for any inquiry into the therapeutic experience itself to be considered meaningful, the employer should take into consideration much more than the employee's satisfaction with the therapist and the counseling experience. Inquiries about such aspects as the therapist's clinical competence, expertise, knowledge, and interpersonal skills should also be made. Outcome evaluations of the clinical/counseling experience should focus on the resolution of the presenting problem and/or the attainment of a specific behavioral goal. Two basic questions must be answered: (1) Has the problem for which the employee initially sought treatment been resolved to his/her satisfaction? (2) Does the employee consider the number of counseling sessions approved for treatment to have been sufficient for resolving the presenting problem to his/her satisfaction?

Finally, the employer must evaluate the performance of the managed mental health care entity in terms of overall cost. When estimating the overall cost of this service, the employer should take into account the two factors discussed below.

Direct Financial Costs

The total sum of all per capita fees paid to the managed mental health care entity for one fiscal year (or for the duration of the contractual agreement) constitutes the actual dollar cost of the program to the employer. Cost-effectiveness can be evaluated simply by comparing this bottom-line figure with the total dollar amount the employer had previously paid to a competing managed care entity or insurance company for comparable mental health care coverage.

Hidden Costs

While the direct costs for using the services of a managed mental health care company are easily determined, the indirect or hidden costs are much more difficult to calculate since they are not readily identifiable. For example, the dollar equivalent for the number of workdays lost to an employer (i.e., due to employee absences, lateness, early departures from the workplace, uncompleted or poorly performed tasks and assignments) caused by psychological problems, emotional stresses, psychosomatic illnesses, family crises, interpersonal difficulties, substance abuse, alcoholism, and so on must also be taken into consideration when one is calculating hidden or unseen costs.

The employer must make sure that any financial savings gained by hiring a particular managed mental health care entity are not offset by decreases in worker productivity that result when the mental health services provided by the managed care company are substandard. For example, let us say that an employer with 1,000 employees contributes $2.50 per employee per month to managed mental health care company A, whose mental health coverage allows each employee to have 30 unmanaged and unrestricted outpatient counseling visits in one calendar year with a copayment of 50% after a $200 deductible. The total direct financial cost to the employer is $2,500 per month, or $30,000 per year. Under this plan, the employer calculates the dollar equivalent for the number of workdays lost (in one calendar year) due to mental health problems to be 200 workdays or 1,600 work hours per year. At an average hourly rate of $8.00, the hidden financial cost incurred by using managed care company A comes to $12,800 per year.

Now let us say that this employer decides to contract with managed mental health care company B for its services since company B requires the employer to contribute only $1.75 per employee per month. The cost to the employer then becomes $1,750 per month, or $21,000 per year. By using managed care company B, therefore, the employer's direct financial cost drops from $30,000 per year to $21,000 per year—a substantial savings of $9,000.

If employees receive the same quality of mental health services from company B as they did from company A, and their coverage and benefits (e.g., premiums, deductibles, copayments, number of unmanaged outpatient visits) remain substantially the same, then both employees and employer will profit from using company B—assuming that hidden costs remain constant. If, however, company B can charge a lower per capita rate than company A only by reducing services, cutting back benefits, and using therapists who are poorly trained and less experienced than those employed by company A, what the employer saves in direct costs may be nullified by increases in hidden or unseen costs. Therefore, evaluation of the success of a managed mental health care entity in actually reducing cost to the employer can be measured only when hidden or unseen costs are subtracted from the bottom line. The following formula should be used by an employer to compare the relative merits of two or more managed mental health care service providers:

$$D \text{ (Direct Costs)} + H \text{ (Hidden Costs)} = A \text{ (Actual Costs)}$$

An employer must be confident that the managed mental health care entity chosen to care for his/her employees' psychological well-being sees its primary responsibility as being the delivery of the most clinically appropriate, least restrictive, and most cost-effective level of care in the most timely and efficient manner possible (Bradman, 1992). The profit motive, for both the employer and the managed mental health care entity, should not take precedence over this primary objective.

The employer must also be sure that the managed mental health care entity selected for the delivery of comprehensive mental health services has the capability to carry out its contractual obligations efficiently, rapidly, consistently, and competently. Bradman (1992) stresses that in order for a managed mental health care entity to offer comprehensive services, it must have in place case management strategies, utilization review procedures, quality assurance practices, benefit administration services, member support systems, claims management capabilities, financial management resources, management information processing systems, and the ongoing development and support of providers and the provider network.

In most businesses, regardless of size, it is unrealistic to expect employers, chief executive officers, benefits managers, human resources personnel, and the like to have the time, knowledge, or expertise required to conduct a thorough empirical evaluation of the managed mental health care services purchased. Therefore, the assistance of independent researchers and consultants is often required. The additional costs involved in hiring these outside consultants must also be taken into account when one calculates overall expenses, i.e., actual costs.

MANAGED CARE'S RESPONSIBILITIES

Contracts, Benefits, and Services

As stated previously, this author agrees with Bradman's axiom that the fundamental purpose of any managed mental health care delivery system should be to provide the highest possible quality care to client beneficiaries in a clinically appropriate way, and in the least restrictive and most cost-effective manner possible. Anything else would be unacceptable. Since the cost of providing managed mental health care services to businesses varies due to factors such as the nature of the benefit package selected by the employer, applicable copayments, deductibles, regional hospital rates, utilization history of the membership, size of population served, and geographical area, the managed mental health care entity has the responsibility to provide ongoing feedback to employers concerning utilization rates and patterns. Bradman (1992) suggests that a provision should exist in the contractual agreement between the managed mental health care company and the employer that allows for a credit to be given to the employer when utilization rates, for a specific period, are significantly lower than predicted. Similarly, in situations where there is unexpectedly high utilization of services, a provision should exist that allows for a reexamination of the rate structure.

A managed mental health care corporation must also offer its clinicians and panel members protection from employer interference with the services they provide to client beneficiaries. In return for such noninterference policies, the managed mental health care entity must agree to conduct outcome assessments of clinical practices and clients' satisfaction with the services they received and to provide the employer with extensive feedback about clinical outcomes and client satisfaction.

The managed mental health care entity must take the responsibility for drawing up clear and straightforward contracts with employers. These contracts, according to some experts, such as Bradman (1992), should specifically list all of the services that are to be provided. The recipients of the services must also be clearly identified (e.g., employees, retirees). Full acknowledgment of the scope and limits of coverage must be clearly delineated. (For example, does the contract include an EAP provision? Is treatment for substance abuse included? Are collateral contacts permitted?)

The managed mental health care entity should also identify any unusual situations or circumstances that might occur, such as when the employer wishes to have additional services provided that are not routinely included in its mental health care benefits package (e.g., marital counseling, family therapy, school consultations, home observations of children's behavior).

The managed care entity must also clarify procedures that will be followed in situations where employees are either in treatment prior to the commencement of a contract or are in need of treatment after the contract terminates. The managed care organization must have procedures and policies in place that allow for the efficient and clinically sound handling of employee/beneficiary transfers and termination of clinical services. Issues related to such considerations as the continuity of care, transfer of records, and confidentiality that might arise during the transition into or out of a contract must be fully addressed. Any possible exceptions, special circumstances, and atypical cases must also be dealt with openly and straightforwardly in the contractual agreement between the managed mental health care entity and the employer.

The managed care entity must make sure that all contracts with employers define the means used to determine eligibility. In cases where an employee is in treatment or requires treatment, but has not yet become eligible for coverage or has lost his/her coverage for some reason, a clear provision should exist for resolving such situations in a timely and effective manner, with minimal inconvenience to the employee/beneficiary.

In addition to the descriptions of services, the contract must clearly address the service areas to be covered and what will happen when a client beneficiary has an emergency outside the service area. A clear and unequivocal definition of an emergency situation is necessary, and the benefits that are available in case of an emergency must also be clearly delineated for the employer (Bradman, 1992).

The managed mental health care entity should also provide the employer and all client beneficiaries with a clear summary of the managed mental health care plan itself. Such a summary should include a carefully worded statement regarding benefit provisions, exclusions, limitations of coverage, and restrictions. It should also list, as precisely as possible, what constitutes covered and noncovered services and to what extent services must undergo authorization or certification processes.

Bradman (1992) suggests that any summary statement about benefits and services should clearly differentiate between mental health and substance abuse services and medical and surgical services. Confusion can arise in situations in which both services are rendered and two diagnoses, one medical and one psychiatric, are appropriate. For example, if inpatient detoxification of a client beneficiary is necessary and the detoxification process is conducted by a medical staff or nonpsychiatric physician, a managed mental health care company may consider this a medical expense to be paid for by the managed health care company responsible for medical coverage. To avoid situations in which client beneficiaries are caught between two managed care companies involved in a claims dispute, a complete and comprehensible definition of what constitutes a medical treatment and what constitutes a mental health or substance abuse treatment should be included in any plan summary.

Managed mental health care entities must also have formal systems and processes in place that are designed specifically to handle all client beneficiaries' grievances. Procedures outlining the grievance process should be made available to employers and employees.

Institutions and Facilities

Managed mental health care entities have the responsibility of maintaining an ongoing and collaborative professional relationship with hospitals and other inpatient facilities that are conveniently located and near the residences of the client beneficiaries they serve. It is the responsibility of the managed mental health care entity to make certain that all inpatient facilities that clients will be expected to use are fully credentialed and accredited. These inpatient facilities should be able to provide all required inpatient services, including transportation services for clients whenever necessary. Further, they should all have a standard procedure in place to handle psychiatric emergencies. When a psychiatric emergency necessitates an admission to an out-of-network inpatient facility, clearly delineated procedures for dealing with such an emergency must be in place. A full discussion of how such emergencies will be handled must be included in any contractual agreement between a managed mental health care entity and an employer.

Facilities representing the entire spectrum of care should be included in the treatment network of any managed mental health care entity. For example, in addition to inpatient facilities, day treatment centers, partial hospitalization programs, detoxification units, halfway houses, and rehabilitation centers should all be available options for clients (Bradman, 1992).

Ethical and Legal Considerations

It is common to find that managed mental health care companies differ widely in the rates they charge employers for services. This is based on the fact that different companies deliver different services. In the marketing of managed mental health care services to employers, managed mental health care companies all stress the quality of the services they are promoting and the cost-effectiveness of their programs. However, from an ethical point of view, these organizations have a duty to explain to employers how they have arrived at the rates they plan to charge for their services.

When a business contracts with a managed mental health care

organization to oversee and micromanage mental health services, it automatically assumes the financial burdens associated with adding a large administrative component to direct service delivery costs. Some of the monies contributed by employers and employees for mental health care that previously would have been used to cover the costs of direct services must now be diverted to pay for administrative overhead expenses and the salaries of nonclinical personnel and persons not directly administering clinical services to client beneficiaries (e.g., corporate officers, boards of directors, contract negotiators, benefits specialists, consultants, accountants, bookkeepers, case managers, review specialists, support staff, and clerical workers). Therefore, the managed mental health care entity should provide the employer with a precise financial breakdown of how all monies contributed to the managed mental health care organization were actually spent. These data should be reported quarterly in a clear and straightforward manner that makes it easy for the employer to compare administrative costs associated with the direct delivery of clinical services.

In this author's opinion, it is unethical for a managed mental health care entity to employ utilization review procedures to restrict, limit, curtail, ration, deny, or in any way prevent client beneficiaries from receiving *the full benefit of contracted-for services* in order to offset administrative expenses or to increase the profits of the managed mental health care company. Similarly, it is unethical, and may actually constitute a civil rights violation, for a managed mental health care company to require client beneficiaries to undergo psychopharmacological treatments in lieu of psychotherapy for the sole purpose of reducing the expense of paying for outpatient visits. A managed mental health care company has a duty to inform an employer if it is company policy to engage in such cost-cutting practices as a way of holding down capitation rates. Employers have the right to know, as well as a duty to investigate, whether the financial savings they stand to gain by using a particular managed mental health care entity will actually be realized at the expense of their employees.

Bradman (1992) recommends that managed mental health care companies seeking to negotiate contracts with businesses should voluntarily supply a list of references to all employers to whom they wish to offer their services. An effective managed mental health care entity should receive endorsements from a variety of sources, for example, benefits consultants, insurers, claims administrators, employers, hospitals, medical directors, local professionals, and union officials.

Clinical Personnel and Clinical Practice

The foundation of a managed mental health care company is its clinical staff. Any managed mental health care entity hoping to do business in a particular geographical area must have an adequate number of seasoned providers who are appropriately dispersed geographically. All providers must be experienced, licensed, insured, and properly credentialed. These providers should be required to render direct services to client beneficiaries and should not be employed simply to supervise less credentialed, inexperienced, or unlicensed practitioners.

Managed mental health care administrators have an obligation to make certain that all individuals involved in the delivery of direct services to client beneficiaries have been adequately trained to deliver these services competently and independently of on-site supervision. In order for a managed mental health care service delivery system to operate at maximum efficiency, the roles and functions of all individuals involved in direct service delivery, and the role relationships between and among them, must be clearly delineated and differentiated. For example, the individuals responsible for telephone intake and screening interviews should not engage in treatment; rather, their primary responsibilities should be (a) to gather relevant information about the nature of the presenting problem so that case managers can make referrals to appropriate providers in the network, and (b) to verify the client beneficiaries' benefits so that both the case manager and the treating therapist have a clear understanding concerning which service plan (i.e., benefits and exclusions) applies to a particular client beneficiary.

The case manager's role and responsibilities vis-à-vis the treating therapist must be clearly defined and understood by both professionals so as to avoid any confusion that might negatively affect the therapeutic relationship. Confusion and conflicts between the treating therapist and the case manager can develop when the case manager assumes the role of clinical supervisor. This type of arrangement is dysfunctional and should be avoided for a number of reasons.

First, in order to supervise another therapist, the case manager must be a well-trained, senior clinician who has specialized in, or who has distinguished himself/herself in, the particular treatment being conducted by the therapist. Unfortunately, this arrangement is not typical in the majority of cases. Frequently, case managers are generalists who have considerably less clinical training, experience, and expertise than the majority of the network providers with whom they work.

Second, even if the case manager were a well-trained, senior clinician with outstanding credentials, most managed mental health care organizations are not set up to offer on-site supervision to providers in their networks. In many instances, the case manager has never seen the client in a face-to-face diagnostic interview. Similarly, the case manager may not even know the treating therapist personally. Such an arrangement does not meet even minimal criteria for a supervisory relationship.

For reasons outlined, it is essential that the case manager's role be one of treatment coordinator rather than clinical supervisor. The task of the case manager should be to gather relevant clinical information that the therapist can use to formulate the most cost-effective treatment plan possible. Decisions about type and length of treatment should be made collaboratively by the therapist and the case manager. The relationship between the treating clinician and the case manager should be collegial rather than adversarial.

A managed mental health care entity has the responsibility for employing clinicians who are truly senior-level practitioners who can advise and supervise less experienced clinicians whenever expert input is required.

Ever since Eysenck (1952) first questioned the effectiveness of traditional psychotherapies, there has been a steady increase in the number and quality of empirical studies designed to assess clinical outcomes. The long history of these investigations is chronicled in a series of scholarly volumes (Bergin & Garfield, 1971, 1994; Garfield & Bergin, 1978, 1986). When one considers the wealth of data collected over the years, it is apparent that individual, group, and marital/family therapies are highly effective in bringing about desired behavioral, cognitive, and affective changes in individuals and marital/family systems, and that these changes tend to be of long duration. However, there are disconcerting empirical findings that document that negative therapeutic reactions, such as worsening of symptoms and client deterioration, also occur as a result of the psychotherapeutic experience. Client deterioration has been shown to be related to therapist incompetence and inexperience.

Given that negative therapeutic consequences do result when poorly prepared, inexperienced, and unqualified practitioners are permitted to engage in psychotherapy and counseling, managed mental health care companies must do all that they can to ensure that all clinicians selected for inclusion in their networks have been adequately trained and sufficiently prepared to conduct the particular forms of therapy they plan to offer clients.

One criterion that is used by many managed mental health care organizations when considering a clinician's suitability for panel inclusion is whether the clinician says that he/she practices brief and/or short-term psychotherapy. Brief and time-limited therapies, although lacking long-term follow-up data, do appear to be valid clinical approaches that can be used to treat specific behavioral problems (Koss & Butcher, 1986). When conducted by experienced and qualified therapists who have had specific training in short-term techniques, brief and short-term individual, group, and marital/family therapies are successful. However, simply limiting or reducing the number of therapy sessions one has with a client or marital/family system does not automatically make one a competent or qualified short-term practitioner. Similarly, truncating an established treatment approach so that it conforms to some arbitrary number of managed mental health care outpatient sessions does not magically transform what a practitioner does into valid and reliable short-term treatment that is clinically sound and cost-effective.

Managed mental health care corporations have a duty to ensure that all therapists who claim to practice brief, short-term, crisis-oriented, or problem-focused therapies have actually had supervised training in one or more empirically tested models of short-term individual, group, or marital/family intervention. Since most brief, short-term, and crisis-oriented models of therapy tend to be behavioral or cognitive-behavioral in their theoretical/clinical orientation, managed mental health care organizations should take the responsibility for seeking out and recruiting providers who have been trained to practice behavioral and cognitive-behavioral therapies.

From this author's perspective, managed mental health care organizations that do not employ a sufficient number of clinicians who are qualified to conduct brief, short-term, behavioral and cognitive-behavioral therapies must take the responsibility for recruiting such individuals and for training existing panel members in these approaches. The training of panel members in short-term and brief behavioral and cognitive-behavioral models should be extensive and ongoing. One-day seminars or didactic lectures presented to panel members by senior practitioners cannot adequately prepare clinicians to utilize brief, short-term, and behavioral models of intervention.

Various therapist characteristics, behaviors, and attitudes have been shown to contribute significantly to positive therapeutic outcomes in numerous empirical studies. Recently, two excellent reviews of this research were published (Beutler, Machado, & Neufeldt, 1994; Orlinsky, Grawe, & Parks, 1994). While the importance of selected therapist traits, behaviors, and attitudes are recognized, these essentials ingredients mean very little if clients are not assured that the material they share with their therapists and the information they disclose during the course of treatment will be kept in strict confidence. Without the assurance of confidentiality between client and therapist, interpersonal trust cannot develop and the success of the treatment will be severely compromised. Therefore, managed mental health care organizations must do all that they can to protect client beneficiaries' privacy. This means that access to clients' files and confidential material must be limited to a very small number of clinically trained professionals.

THERAPISTS' RESPONSIBILITIES

Clinicians who choose to become members of provider panels owe their first allegiance to the client beneficiaries with whom they work. Panel members must never compromise their professional integrity in order to accommodate the needs of a managed mental health care corporation. For example, clinicians must make sure that they have been adequately trained to conduct the types of treatments that managed mental health care entities will expect them to practice. It is clearly unethical for a clinician to agree to engage in psychotherapeutic practices, testing procedures, or diagnostic assessments for which he/she has not been adequately trained and is not properly credentialed, certified, and licensed.

If a therapist becomes a member of a managed mental health care organization's panel of providers and later discovers that he/she does not have sufficient training to engage in some of the treatments he/she is being asked to conduct, the therapist should inform the case manager about this skills deficit and should refrain from accepting those types of referrals. If the therapist plans to pursue additional training to become qualified to practice the treatments in question, the therapist should tell the case manager about this intention to get remedial training. Once the training and supervision necessary for independent practice have been completed, the therapist should inform the case manager that he/she is ready to accept such referrals.

Throughout this text, the case examples presented for illustration have dealt with managed mental health care organizations that permit a limited number of collateral contacts for the treatment of distressed marriages and family systems of client beneficiaries. However, many mental health care entities do not negotiate contracts that allow for the treatment of V-code conditions. These conditions include marital, family, and child-related problems. Therapists who are panel members of managed health care organizations that do not permit collateral contacts for V-code conditions should be aware of some of the ethical and legal issues that may arise if certain clinical procedures are not followed.

For example, if a client contacts an intake specialist or case manager seeking help for marital, family, or child-related problems, the managed mental health care representative must let the client know immediately whether his/her particular contract allows for collateral contacts. If the client beneficiary's coverage does allow for limited collateral involvements, the managed mental health care representative must inform him/her that such is the case. If, on the other hand, the client's contract does not allow for the collateral involvements of other family members, the intake specialist or case manager must refer the client to an appropriate out-of-network therapist or agency that does offer the services requested.

It is unethical for a case manager or intake specialist to refer a client for individual treatment when the treatment of record for the presenting problem is either marital or family therapy. Furthermore, it is the therapist's duty to inform the client that the treatment of choice for the presenting problem is either marital or family therapy. The therapist must then make the proper referral. If, for some reason, the client chooses to enter individual treatment, the therapist's duty is to inform the client that individual treatment may negatively affect his/her marriage. To withhold this information from a client is unethical and may be considered illegal in some states.

Some managed mental health care organizations that do not recognize marital and family intervention as a legitimately covered mental health benefit still will not allow a therapist to treat a client beneficiary's spouse or child. The policy is to refer any family members to another therapist in the network. From a marital/family systems perspective, such a policy not only fragments the treatment, it also fragments the family. Since the treatment of choice for marital problems and family problems is marital/family therapy, referring a spouse or a child to another therapist could be detrimental to marital stability and family cohesion.

Here again, the therapist's duty is to inform the client beneficiary that the procedures specified by the managed mental health care entity may have deleterious effects on his/her marriage or family. Some legal scholars (Appelbaum, 1993) have suggested that in cases where a managed care organization fails to act reasonably to avoid causing harm to beneficiaries, it is the therapist's responsibility to act as an advocate for the client. If this is not done, it might be considered professional negligence, and the therapist may be held liable for failure to act on behalf of the client beneficiary.

OUTCOME EVALUATIONS

The final issue to be addressed in this chapter on accountability deals with outcome effectiveness and the responsibility of managed mental health care to evaluate the success of its clinical endeavors. In order to get a well-rounded and comprehensive appraisal of therapeutic effectiveness, outcome success should be measured from three perspectives: the client beneficiary's perspective, the therapist's perspective, and an objective third party's perspective. Outcome evaluations should be conducted immediately, at the end of treatment, during a posttreatment assessment session. Follow-up evaluations are also necessary in order to determine the degree and extent to which gains and improvements made during the treatment process are being maintained once formal intervention has been discontinued. Ideally, follow-up evaluations should be conducted at four-month intervals for an entire year.

The person best qualified to judge the effectiveness, success, or failure of any psychotherapeutic intervention is the client beneficiary himself/herself. This first-hand, "insider's view" is indispensable. However, if such evaluations are simply open-ended, non-standardized, self-reports of satisfaction, an objective appraisal of therapeutic outcome cannot be obtained. The reliability and validity of such reports are suspect, since the feelings of clients about their therapists will definitely color their judgments. For example, a couple's positive feelings about their therapist may cause them to rate their therapeutic experience as having been highly successful, even though a third-party case manager or review specialist may record no observable behavior changes in the client's presenting problem (i.e., the husband is still depressed, has little sexual desire, and takes no initiative in his relationship with his wife).

Conversely, positive therapeutic outcomes and quantifiable behavior changes sometimes occur even though one spouse or family member expresses intense dislike for the therapist and considers the therapy to have been a total failure (e.g., a spouse who resents a therapist for having set limits on his/her assaultive, violent, and abusive behavior or a teenager who detests a family therapist who has been successful in teaching his parents how to resolve long-standing marital difficulties so that they are finally able to function as a more efficient parental team that can no longer be manipulated by him). Such subjective evaluations can be put in their proper perspective only if they are complemented by more objective measures and behavioral reports that specifically target the problem behaviors for which collateral contacts had been approved.

Unstructured, open-ended, and subjective self-reports of client beneficiaries' satisfaction and therapeutic outcome certainly have their place in managed mental health care settings, but they should never be the sole source of accountability, especially if no distinction is made between liking one's therapist and actual behavior change, problem resolution, symptom reduction, and so forth.

Unstructured and nonstandardized "outsider" evaluations of therapeutic progress are likewise subject to observer/evaluator bias. This is especially true if the treating therapist is considered an "outsider." Early on in the research studies designed to evaluate psychotherapeutic outcome, researchers questioned the validity and reliability of therapists' reports of their own success, their clients' improvements, and actual behavior changes (e.g., Bergin & Garfield, 1971; Garfield & Bergin, 1978, 1986; Greenberg & Pinsof, 1986; Gurman & Razin, 1977).

In reality, therefore, it can be argued that the therapist is not an objective outsider and that therapists' appraisals of their own effectiveness should actually be treated as subjective "insiders'" evaluations. Like the subjective reports of client beneficiaries, therapists' reports of psychotherapeutic outcome must be balanced by more objective outcome measures. Training in the use of behavioral rating scales will be helpful for clinicians who work in managed care settings since such training will enable them to provide case managers and review specialists with more objective evaluations of their work.

One way to improve the validity and reliability of both clients' and therapists' evaluations of clinical outcome is to teach therapists (who then can teach their clients) how to observe, record, track, monitor, and measure actual behavior changes as they occur in response to specific interventions. When behavioral reports such as these are used in conjunction with other reliable and valid measures of clients' presenting problems (e.g., depression, anxiety, stress, anger, guilt, marital satisfaction, spousal intimacy, sexual satisfaction, spousal cohesion, differentiation from one's family of origin, family enmeshment), a more comprehensive and dynamic picture of change and clinical effectiveness can emerge. For example, notice the differences between the two client beneficiary/therapist accounts of collateral therapy presented in the following examples.

Example I

Husband: I really liked our therapist. He was warm, caring, sensitive, and sincere. He helped us learn how to communicate our feelings to each other and how to listen to each other. I feel less depressed and more hopeful about my marriage now, and more satisfied with my wife.

Wife: I thought the counseling went very well. I liked my therapist. He seemed to understand our problems very well. My husband and I get along better now, and we don't fight as much as we did before we went into counseling. My husband seems happier and I feel less nervous.

Therapist: Mr. Jones appears less depressed than he was when I first saw him one year ago. Marital therapy seems to have helped considerably. He and Mrs. Jones appear to be happier and report fewer conflicts in their marriage now.

Example II

Husband: During the first week of baseline data collection, I recorded an average of 35 irrational beliefs per day.

These irrational beliefs usually served as triggers for my depression. Now, after 10 weeks of cognitive-behavioral therapy and assertiveness training, the number of irrational beliefs averages only two or three per day.

In conjunction with individual therapy, my wife and I began marital therapy. After eight weeks of marital therapy, which consisted of training in communication, conflict negotiation, and problem solving, serious arguments between me and my wife decreased from an average of five or six per week to about one a week. In the last two weeks, we have had only one minor disagreement.

Our sexual relationship has also improved as a result of marital/sex therapy. The frequency of our lovemaking has increased from an average of twice a month, during the baseline period, to an average of two or three times a week.

Wife: After my husband had had about four weeks of individual therapy, I noticed that he seemed less depressed, and I began to feel less anxious about him and his emotional condition. The first week we began having marital therapy, the average number of anxiety-producing irrational beliefs I recorded was nine per day. As of last week, this daily average had dropped to two or three per day.

The frequency of our lovemaking has also gone up since we began sex therapy training. During the baseline period, we had sex only twice a month. Now we have sex an average of two or three times a week. My husband is much more sexually assertive now than he was when we began sex therapy. Before therapy, he rarely initiated sexual relations. Now he takes the initiative at least once a week.

Therapist: This client was initially seen on 10/1/93 for a diagnostic evaluation. He was diagnosed as suffering from a Dysthymic Disorder—DSM-IV 300.40. A program of cognitive behavior therapy was begun. This program consisted of a combination of individual, marital, and sex therapy. During the initial interview, the client received a score of 50 on the Beck Depression Inventory (Beck, 1978). During the first week of baseline data collection, the client reported an average of 35 irrational beliefs per day using the Irrational Beliefs Test (Jones, 1968). These irrational beliefs were said to serve as triggers for the client's depression.

During the second week of treatment, a cognitive behavior therapy program was begun. The treatments included a combination of interventions, (e.g., relaxation, 'stop think' procedures, cognitive restructuring, and assertiveness training).

A number of the client's irrational beliefs had to do with his relationship with his wife and their marriage. Therefore, during the third week of treatment, marital/sex therapy was introduced as an adjunct to individual work.

After nine weeks of combined treatment, the client reported the number of irrational beliefs that typically sparked depression to have dropped to an average of two or three per day. The client's score on the Beck Depression Inventory at this time was 17.

Cognitive-behavioral marital and sex therapy as outlined by Bagarozzi and Anderson (1989) was instituted during the fourth week of treatment. The following instruments were used to assess pretreatment/posttreatment levels of distress and dysfunction: Locke-Wallace Marital Adjustment Test (Locke & Wallace, 1959), the Pragmatic Marital Assessment Questionnaire (see pp. 45–50), the Index of Sexual Satisfaction (Hudson, Harrison, & Grosscup, 1981), and the Golombok-Rust Inventory of Sexual Satisfaction (Golombok, Rust, & Pickard, 1984).

The couple was taught functional communication

skills, conflict negotiation skills, and problem-solving skills, and a sensate focus regimen was prescribed.

In the second example, we can see that the behavioral reports made by the therapist are very similar to the behavioral self-reports and observations made by the client and his spouse. These self-reports, coupled with the pretreatment/posttreatment scores obtained on individual measures and marital assessment instruments, provide a much more objective picture of therapeutic changes in the identified patient. The wife's behavioral report of her husband's depression also serves as an "outsider's" assessment of the client's progress in individual therapy.

Follow-up evaluations are essential for determining the degree to which cognitive, affective, and behavioral changes made in therapy are maintained once formal treatment has been discontinued. Administration of the same instruments used in pretreatment assessment and posttreatment outcome evaluation at four-month intervals for a period of one year will provide the therapist and managed mental health care personnel with objective data concerning the long-term effects of treatment. In addition to these standardized instruments, the author has developed a brief follow-up questionnaire. This questionnaire is treatment-method specific. Each client is asked to rate core aspects of treatment, such as resolution of the presenting problem, symptom modification, and specific behavioral changes. In addition, clients are asked to assess the level of improvement and the maintenance of specific behavioral gains. In treatments where specific skills are taught, clients are asked to rate the degree to which these skills were learned and whether they still use these skills in their everyday lives. The questionnaires for individuals, couples, and families are presented next.

FOLLOW-UP QUESTIONNAIRE

Individual Treatment

1. If you sought individual psychotherapy for the relief of a specific symptom (e.g., anxiety, depression, guilt feelings,

unresolved grief reaction, anger, low self-esteem, under-assertiveness, low sexual desire, obsessive thoughts, compulsive behaviors, or another specific symptom), please specify the symptom_____; what degree of improvement did you experience by the end of treatment? Please circle one response:

Slight improvement				*Moderate improvement*				*A great deal of improvement*	
1	2	3	4	5	6	7	8	9	10

2. How do you rate the level of improvement for this same symptom or behavior *today*? Please circle one response:

    (a) The level of improvement has remained essentially the same.
    (b) The level of improvement has increased.
    (c) The level of improvement has decreased.
    (d) The symptom or behavior has returned.

3. If you did not seek help for a specific symptom or problem behavior, but sought help with interpersonal relationships with friends, relatives, business associates, etc., to what degree had these relationships improved by the end of our work in therapy? Please circle one response:

Slight improvement				*Moderate improvement*				*A great deal of improvement*	
1	2	3	4	5	6	7	8	9	10

4. As a result of our work in therapy, how much understanding and insight did you develop into the nature of these problems by the end of therapy? Pleases circle one response:

Little understanding				*Moderate understanding*				*A great deal of understanding*	
1	2	3	4	5	6	7	8	9	10

5. To what degree have you been able to use this understanding, knowledge, and insight to improve your current interpersonal relationships? Please circle one response:

Very little				*A moderate amount*				*A great deal*	
1	2	3	4	5	6	7	8	9	10

Marital/Couple Therapy

6. If you sought help *with a partner* for a marital or relationship problem, to what degree do you think you learned to use the following skills by the end of treatment? Please circle one response for each skill:

	Very little				*A moderate amount*				*A great deal*	
(a) Functional communication	1	2	3	4	5	6	7	8	9	10
(b) Problem solving	1	2	3	4	5	6	7	8	9	10
(c) Conflict negotiation	1	2	3	4	5	6	7	8	9	10
(d) Compromise	1	2	3	4	5	6	7	8	9	10
(e) Empathy (understanding your partner's feelings)	1	2	3	4	5	6	7	8	9	10
(f) Role taking (understanding how your partner perceives and experiences you)	1	2	3	4	5	6	7	8	9	10

7. To what extent do you and your partner use these same skills *today*? Please circle one response for each skill:

	Very little	A moderate amount	A great deal
(a) Functional communication	1 2 3 4 5 6 7 8 9 10		
(b) Problem solving	1 2 3 4 5 6 7 8 9 10		
(c) Conflict negotiation	1 2 3 4 5 6 7 8 9 10		
(d) Compromise	1 2 3 4 5 6 7 8 9 10		
(e) Empathy (understanding your partner's feelings)	1 2 3 4 5 6 7 8 9 10		
(f) Role taking (understanding how your partner perceives and experiences you)	1 2 3 4 5 6 7 8 9 10		

8. By the end of treatment, how satisfied were you with your partner? Circle one response:

Not at all satisfied				Moderately satisfied				Very satisfied	
1	2	3	4	5	6	7	8	9	10

9. How satisfied are you *today* with your partner? Please circle one response:

Not at all satisfied				Moderately satisfied				Very satisfied	
1	2	3	4	5	6	7	8	9	10

10. By the end of treatment, how satisfied were you with your marriage? Please circle one response:

Not at all satisfied				*Moderately satisfied*				*Very satisfied*	
1	2	3	4	5	6	7	8	9	10

11. How satisfied are you *today* with your marriage? Please circle one response:

Not at all satisfied				*Moderately satisfied*				*Very satisfied*	
1	2	3	4	5	6	7	8	9	10

Family Therapy

12. If you sought help for a family problem and were seen in conjunction with other family members, to what extent was the problem (that brought you into therapy) resolved by the end of treatment? Please circle one response:

Slightly resolved				*Moderately resolved*				*Completely resolved*	
1	2	3	4	5	6	7	8	9	10

13. How do you rate the level of improvement for this same problem *today*? Please circle one response:

   (a) The level of improvement has remained essentially the same.
   (b) The level of improvement has increased.
   (c) The level of improvement has decreased.
   (d) The problem has returned.

14. To what degree do you think you learned to use the following skills by the end of our family work? Please circle one response for each skill:

	Very little		A moderate amount		A great deal
(a) Functional communication	1 2 3 4 5 6 7 8 9 10				
(b) Problem solving	1 2 3 4 5 6 7 8 9 10				
(c) Conflict negotiation	1 2 3 4 5 6 7 8 9 10				
(d) Compromise	1 2 3 4 5 6 7 8 9 10				
(e) Empathy (understanding the feelings of other family members)	1 2 3 4 5 6 7 8 9 10				
(f) Role taking (understanding how other family members perceive and experience you)	1 2 3 4 5 6 7 8 9 10				

15. To what extent do you use these same skills *today* in your relationships with other family members? Please circle one response for each skill:

	Very little		A moderate amount		A great deal
(a) Functional communication	1 2 3 4 5 6 7 8 9 10				
(b) Problem solving	1 2 3 4 5 6 7 8 9 10				
(c) Conflict negotiation	1 2 3 4 5 6 7 8 9 10				
(d) Compromise	1 2 3 4 5 6 7 8 9 10				
(e) Empathy (understanding the feelings of other family members)	1 2 3 4 5 6 7 8 9 10				

	Very little	A moderate amount	A great deal

   f) Role taking (understanding how other
family members
perceive and
experience you)   1 2 3 4 5 6 7 8 9 10

16. By the end of treatment, how satisfied were you with how
your family solved problems and functioned as a unit?
Please circle one response:

Not at all satisfied				Moderately satisfied				Very satisfied	
1	2	3	4	5	6	7	8	9	10

17. How satisfied are you *today* with how your family solves
problems and functions as a unit? Please circle one response:

Not at all satisfied				Moderately satisfied				Very satisfied	
1	2	3	4	5	6	7	8	9	10

18. What aspects of therapy and the therapist's behavior do
you believe to have been the least helpful? Please explain
your answer and give suggestions for improvement below:

19. What aspects of therapy and the therapist's behavior do
you believe to have been the most helpful? Please explain
your answer below:

This chapter has focused on some of the salient ethical issues that one must consider when evaluating the cost and overall effectiveness of a managed mental health care service delivery system. The future and viability of managed mental health care companies in the United States will depend, to a large degree, on the ability of managed mental health care corporations to demonstrate that their clinical practitioners are competent to provide high-quality, yet cost-effective, short-term mental health and psychological services to the client beneficiaries they serve.

Subjective anecdotal treatment reports and clinical summaries that claim success (no matter how skillfully written) and outcome measures that lack empirical validity (no matter how convincing their face validity) will not be sufficient to satisfy beneficiaries and independent evaluators (e.g., consumer protection groups, members of the major mental health professions). For accountability to be demonstrated satisfactorily, managed mental health care providers and their therapists will have to document their effectiveness by using universally accepted scientific research methods and evaluation procedures. It is hoped that this text will help to facilitate that process.

References

Anderson, R.P., & Anderson, G.V. (1962). Development of an instrument for measuring rapport. In L. Litwack, R. Getson, & G. Saltzman (Eds.), *Research in counseling* (pp. 4–8). Itasco, IL: Peacock.

Appelbaum, P.S. (1993). Legal liability and managed care. *American Psychologist, 48,* 251–257.

Bagarozzi, D.A. (1980a). Holistic family therapy and clinical supervision: Systems, behavioral and psychoanalytic perspectives. *Family Therapy, 2,* 153–165.

Bagarozzi, D.A. (1980b). *Functional communication and conflict negotiation adequacy checklist.* Unpublished instrument. Atlanta: Human Resources Consultants.

Bagarozzi, D.A. (1983a). A cognitive-sociobehavioral model of clinical social work practice and evaluation. *Clinical Social Work Journal, 11,* 164–177.

Bagarozzi, D.A. (1983b). Methodological developments in measuring social exchange perceptions in marital dyads (SIDCARB): A new tool for clinical intervention. In D.A. Bagarozzi, A.P. Jurich, & R.W. Jackson (Eds.), *New perspectives in marital and family therapy: Issues in theory, research and practice* (pp. 79–104). New York: Human Sciences Press.

Bagarozzi, D.A. (1983c). Contingency contracting for structural and process changes in family systems. In L.A. Wolberg & M.L. Aronson (Eds.), *Group and family therapy 1983: An overview.* New York: Brunner/Mazel.

147

Bagarozzi, D.A. (1985). Dimensions of family evaluation. In L. L'Abate (Ed.), *Handbook of family psychology* (pp. 989–1005). Homewood, IL: Dorsey Press.

Bagarozzi, D.A. (1989). Family diagnostic testing: A neglected area of expertise for the family psychologist. *American Journal of Family Therapy, 17,* 261–274.

Bagarozzi, D.A. (1990). *Intimacy needs survey.* Unpublished instrument. Atlanta: Human Resources Consultants.

Bagarozzi, D.A. (1992a). *Pragmatic marital assessment questionnaire.* Unpublished instrument. Atlanta: Human Resources Consultants.

Bagarozzi, D.A. (1992b). Clinical uses and limitations of social exchange principles. In P. Boss, W. Doherty, R. LaRosa, W. Schumm, & S. Steinmetz (Eds.), *Sourcebook of family theories and methods* (pp. 412–418). New York: Plenum.

Bagarozzi, D.A., & Anderson, S.A. (1989). *Personal, marital and family myths: Theoretical formulations and clinical strategies.* New York: Norton.

Bagarozzi, D.A., & Giddings, C.W. (1982). Family therapy with violent families. *American Journal of Family Therapy, 10,* 69–72.

Bagarozzi, D.A., & Giddings, C.W. (1983). Conjugal violence: A critical review of research and clinical practices. *American Journal of Family Therapy, 11,* 3–15.

Barrett-Lennard, G.T. (1962). Dimensions of therapists' responses as causal factors in therapeutic change. *Psychological Monographs, 76,* (43 whole no. 562).

Bateson, G. (1935). Culture, contact and schismogenesis. *Man, 35,* 178–183.

Bateson, G. (1936). *Naven.* Cambridge, England: Cambridge University Press.

Bateson, G. (1972). *Steps to an ecology of the mind.* New York: Ballantine Books.

Beavers, W.R., Hampson, R.B., & Hulgus, Y.F. (1985). The Beavers system approach to family assessment. *Family Process, 24,* 398–405.

Beck, A.T. (1978). *Beck depression inventory.* Philadelphia: Center for Cognitive Therapy.

Bergin, A.E., & Garfield, S.L. (Eds.). (1971). *Handbook of psychotherapy and behavior change* (1st ed.). New York: Wiley.

Bergin, A.E., & Garfield, S.L. (Eds.). (1994). *Handbook of psychotherapy and behavior change* (4th ed.). New York: Wiley.

Beutler, L.E., Machado, P.P., & Neufeldt, S.A. (1994). Therapist variables. In A.E. Bergin & S.L. Garfield (Eds.), *Handbook of psychotherapy and behavior change* (4th ed.) (pp. 229–269). New York: Wiley.

Bradman, L.H. (1992). *Managed mental health care: The Bradman approach.* Plantation, FL: Unipsych Press.

Brantley, P.J., Cocke, T.B., Jones, G.N., & Goreczny, A.J. (1988). The daily stress inventory: Validity and effect of repeated administration. *Journal of Psychopathology and Behavioral Assessment, 10,* 75–81.

Brantley, P.J., & Jones, G.N. (1989). *Daily stress inventory: Professional manual.* Odessa, FL: Psychological Assessment Resources.

Bray, J., Williamson, D., & Malone, P. (1984). Personal authority in the family system: Development of a questionnaire to measure personal authority in intergenerational family processes. *Journal of Marital and Family Therapy, 10,* 167–178.

Cook, D.R. (1989). *Internalized shame scale.* Menomonie, WI: University of Wisconsin.

Dell, P.F. (1983). Researching the family theories of schizophrenia: An exercise in epistemological confusion. In D.A. Bagarozzi, A.P. Jurich, & R.W. Jackson (Eds.), *Marital and family therapy: New perspectives in theory, research and practice* (pp. 236–261). New York: Human Sciences Press.

Digran, M., & Anspaugh, D. (1978). Permissiveness and premarital sexual activity: Behavioral correlates of attitudinal differences. *Adolescence, 13,* 703–711.

Ericson, P.M., & Rogers, L.E. (1973). New procedures for analyzing relational communication. *Family Process, 12,* 244–267.

Eysenck, H.J. (1952). The effects of psychotherapy: An evaluation. *Journal of Consulting Psychology, 16,* 319–324.

Garfield, S.L., & Bergin, A.E. (Eds.). (1978). *Handbook of psychotherapy and behavior change: An empirical analysis* (2nd ed.). New York: Wiley.

Garfield, S.L., & Bergin, A.E. (Eds.). (1986). *Handbook of psychotherapy and behavior change: An empirical analysis* (3rd ed.). New York: Wiley.

Golombok, R., Rust, J., & Pickard, C. (1984). Sexual problems encountered in general practice. *British Journal of Sexual Medicine, 11,* 65–72.

Greenberg, L.S., & Pinsof, W.M. (Eds.). (1986). *The psychotherapeutic process: A research handbook.* New York: Guilford.

Gurman A. S., & Kniskern, D. P. (1981). *Handbook of family therapy.* New York: Brunner/Mazel.

Gurman A.S., & Kniskern, D.P., & Pinsof, W.M. (1986). Research on marital and family therapies. In S.L. Garfield & A.E. Bergin (Eds.), *Handbook of psychotherapy and behavior change* (3rd ed.) (pp. 565–626). New York: Wiley.

Gurman A.S., & Razin, A.M. (Eds.). (1977). *Effective psychotherapy: A handbook of research*. New York: Pergamon.

Haley, J. (1963). Marriage therapy. *Archives of General Psychiatry, 8,* 213–224.

Hovestadt, A.J., Anderson, W.T., Piercy, F.P., Cochran, S.W., & Fine, M. (1985). A family-of-origin scale. *Journal of Marriage and Family Therapy, 15,* 19–27.

Hudson, W.W., Harrison, D.F., & Grosscup, P.C. (1981). A short-term scale to measure sexual discord in dyadic relationships. *Journal of Sex Research, 17,* 157–174.

Jackson, D.D. (1959). Family interaction, family homeostasis and some implications for conjoint family psychotherapy. In J. Masserman (Ed.), *Individual and family dynamics*. New York: Grune & Stratton.

Jackson, D.D. (1965). Family rules: Marital quid pro quo. *Archives of General Psychiatry, 12,* 589–594.

Jackson, D.D., & Lederer, W. (1968). *The mirages of marriage*. New York: Norton.

Janda, L.H., & O'Grady, K.E. (1980). Development of a sex anxiety inventory. *Journal of Consulting and Clinical Psychology, 48,* 169–175.

Joaning, H., & Kuehl, B. (1986). Family adaptability and cohesion scales III: A review. *American Journal of Family Therapy, 14,* 163–165.

Jones, R.G. (1968). A factored measure of Ellis' irrational beliefs system. Wichita, KS: Test Systems, Inc.

Jordan, T.J., & McCormick, N.B. (1988). Development of a measure of irrational beliefs about sex. *Journal of Sex Education and Therapy, 14,* 28–32.

Keeney, B.P. (1982). What is an epistemology of family therapy? *Family Process, 21,* 153–168.

Koss, M.P., & Butcher, J.N. (1986). Research on brief psychotherapy. In S.L. Garfield & A.E. Bergin (Eds.), *Handbook of psychotherapy and behavior change* (3rd ed.) (pp. 627–670). New York: Wiley.

Krug, S.E., Scheier, I. H., & Cattell, R.B. (1976). *Anxiety scale questionnaire*. Champaign, IL: Institute for Personality and Ability Testing.

L'Abate, L. (1976). *Understanding and helping the individual in the family*. New York: Grune & Stratton.

L'Abate, L. (1977). *Enrichment: Structured programs for couples, families and groups*. Washington, DC: University Press of America.

L'Abate, L. (1981). Skills training programs for couples and families: Clinical and nonclinical applications. In A.S. Gurman & D.P. Kniskern (Eds.), *Handbook of family therapy*. New York: Brunner/Mazel.

L'Abate, L., & Bagarozzi, D.A. (1993). *Sourcebook of marriage and family evaluation*. New York: Brunner/Mazel.

Lewis, J.M., Beavers, W.R., Gossett, J.T., & Phillips, V.A. (1976). *No single thread: Psychological health in family systems.* New York: Brunner/Mazel.

Libby, R.W. (1971). Parental attitudes toward high school sex education programs: Liberalism–traditionalism and demographic correlates. *Family Coordinator, 20,* 127–136.

Locke, H.J., & Wallace, K.M. (1959). Short marital adjustment and prediction test: Their reliability and validity. *Marriage and Family Living,* 251–255.

McCubbin, H.I., Olson, D.H., & Larsen, A.S. (1987). *F-COPES: Family crisis oriented personal evaluation scales.* In H.I. McCubbin & A.I. Thompson (Eds.), *Family assessment inventories for research and practice* (pp. 259–270). Madison, WI: University of Wisconsin–Madison, Family Stress Coping and Health Project.

McCubbin, H.I., & Patterson, J.M. (1987). FILE: *Family inventory of life events and changes.* In H.I. McCubbin & A.I. Thompson (Eds.), *Family assessment inventories for research and practice* (pp. 81–98). Madison, WI: University of Wisconsin–Madison, Family Stress Coping and Health Project.

Mead, D.E., Vatcher, G.M., Wyne, B.A., & Roberts, S.L. (1990). The comprehensive areas of change questionnaire: Assessing marital couples' presenting complaints. *American Journal of Family Therapy, 18,* 65–79.

Moos, R.H., & Moos, B.S. (1981). *Family environment scale manual.* Palo Alto, CA: Consulting Psychologist Press.

Mosher, D.L. (1966). The development of a multitract-multimethod matrix analysis of three measures and three aspects of guilt. *Journal of Consulting and Clinical Psychology, 30,* 35–39.

Mosher, D.L. (1968). Measurement of guilt in females by self report inventories. *Journal of Consulting and Clinical Psychology, 32,* 690–695.

Murstein, B.I., Cerreto, M., & MacDonald, M. (1977). A theory and investigation of the effect of exchange orientation on marriage and friendship. *Journal of Marriage and the Family, 39,* 543–549.

Obler, M. (1973). Systematic desensitization in sexual disorders. *Journal of Behavior Therapy and Experiment Psychiatry, 4,* 93–101.

Olson, D.H., & Barnes, H.L. (1982). *Quality of life questionnaire.* In D.H. Olson, H.L. McCubbin, H. Barnes, A. Larsen, M. Muxen, & M. Wilson (Eds.), *Family inventories* (pp. 147–148). St. Paul, MN: University of Minnesota, Family Social Science.

Olson, D.H., Portner, J., & Lavee, Y. (1985). *FACES III.* St. Paul, MN: University of Minnesota.

Orlinsky, D.E., Grawe, K., & Parks, B.K. (1994). Process and outcome in psychotherapy—Noch Einmal. In A.E. Bergin & S.L. Garfield (Eds.), *Handbook of psychotherapy and behavior change* (4th ed.) (pp. 270–378). New York: Wiley.

Patterson, D.G., & O'Gorman, E.C. (1986). The SOMA: A questionnaire measure of sex and anxiety. *British Journal of Psychiatry, 4,* 93–101.

Reynolds, W.M. (1991). *Adult suicidal ideation questionnaire.* Odessa, FL: Assessment Resources.

Rogers, L.E. & Bagarozzi, D.A. (1983). An overview of relational communication and implications for therapy. In D.A. Bagarozzi, A.P. Jurich, & R.W. Jackson (Eds.), *New perspectives in marital and family therapy: Issues in theory, research and practice* (pp. 48–78). New York: Human Sciences Press.

Rogers, L.E., Courtright, J.A., & Millar, F.E. (1982). Message control intensity: Rationale and preliminary findings. *Communication Monographs,* 1982.

Sabatelli, R.M. (1988). Personal authority in the family systems questionnaire (PAFS-Q): A review. *American Journal of Family Therapy, 16,* 167–170.

Schiavi, R.C., Derogatis, L.R., Kuriansky, J., O'Connor, D., & Sharpe, L. (1979). The assessment of sexual functioning and marital interaction. *Journal of Sex and Marital Therapy, 18,* 179–224.

Schumm, W.R., Jurich, A.P., & Bollman, S.R. (1986). Kansas marital satisfaction scale. Manhattan, KS: Kansas State University.

Spanier, G. (1976). Measuring dyadic adjustment: New scales for assessing the quality of marriage and similar dyads. *Journal of Marriage and the Family, 38,* 15–30.

Spielberger, C.D. (1991). *State-trait anger expression inventory: Professional manual.* Odessa, FL: Psychological Assessment Resources.

Straus, M.A. (1979). Measuring intrafamilial conflict and violence: The conflict tactics (CT) scales. *Journal of Marriage and the Family, 41,* 75–88.

Strayhorn, J.M. (1978). Social exchange theory: Cognitive restructuring in marital therapy. *Family Process, 17,* 437–448.

Stuart, R.B., & Jacobson, N. (1991). *Couples precounseling inventory: Psychometric properties and norms.* Seattle, WA: University of Washington, Center for the Study of Relationships.

Stuart, R.B., & Stuart, F. (1980). *Premarital counseling inventory, family precounseling inventory program and marital precounseling inventory.* Champaign, IL: Research Press.

Watzlawick, P., Beavin, J.H., & Jackson, D.D. (1967). *Pragmatics of human communication.* New York: Norton.

Weis, D.L., Slosnerick, M., Cate, R., & Sollie, D.L. (1986). A survey instrument for assessing the cognitive association of sex, love, and marriage. *Journal of Sex Research, 22,* 206–220.

Weiss, R.L., & Birchler, G.R. (1983). *Areas of change questionnaire.* Eugene, OR: University of Oregon.

Weiss, R.L., & Summers, K.J. (1983). Marital interaction coding system III. In E.E. Filsinger (Ed.), *Marriage and family assessment* (pp. 85–115). Beverly Hills, CA: Sage.

Yourglich, A. (1966). Constructing a sibling system measurement device. *Family Coordinator, 15,* 107–111.

Name Index

A

Anderson, G. V., 95
Anderson, R. P., 95
Anderson, S. A., viii, 4, 14, 18, 25, 30, 79, 94, 138
Anderson, W. T., 24, 92
Anspaugh, D., 24
Appelbaum, P. S., 10, 133

B

Bagarozzi, D. A., viii, 1, 4, 14, 18, 23, 25, 26, 27, 30, 31, 32, 38, 39, 40, 41, 42, 44, 45, 79, 81, 82, 94, 103, 111, 138
Barnes, H. L., 85
Barrett-Lennard, G. T., 95
Bateson, G., 14
Beavers, W. R., 27, 45
Beavin, J. H., 11, 14
Beck, A. T., 16, 59, 60, 85
Bergin, A. E., 130, 135
Beutler, L. E., 130
Birchler, G. R., 43
Bollman, S. R., 38

Bradman, L. H., 122, 123, 124, 125, 126, 127
Brantley, P. J., 60
Bray, J., 24, 92, 111
Butcher, J. N., 130

C

Cate, R., 24
Cattell, R. B., 99, 112
Cerreto, M., 26, 43, 44
Cochran, S. W., 24, 92
Cocke, T. B., 60
Cook, D. R., 24

D

Dell, P. F., 28
Derogatis, L. R., 24
Digran, M., 24

E

Ericson, P. M., 15, 27, 45
Eysenck, H. J., 129

155

F

Fine, M., 24, 92

G

Garfield, S. L., 130, 135
Giddings, C. W., 44, 81, 82
Golombok, R., 138
Goreczny, A. J., 60
Grawe, K., 130
Greenberg, L. S., 135
Grosscup, P. C., 138
Gurman, A. S., 25, 78, 135

H

Haley, J., 11, 14, 17
Hampson, R. B., 27, 45
Harrison, D. F., 138
Hovestadt, A. J., 24, 92
Hudson, W. W., 138
Hulgus, Y. F., 27, 45

J

Jackson, D. D., 11, 14, 43
Jacobson, N., 42
Janda, L. H., 24
Joanning, H., 39
Jones, G. N., 60
Jordan, T. J., 24
Jurich, A. P., 38

K

Keeney, B. P., 28
Kniskern, D. P., 25, 78
Koss, M. P., 130
Krug, S. E., 99, 112
Kuehl, B., 39
Kuriansky, J., 24

L

L'Abate, L., viii, 14, 23, 29, 31, 39, 41,
    111
Larsen, A. S., 85
Lavee, Y., 26, 39, 41
Lederer, W., 43
Libby, R. W., 24
Locke, H. J., 26, 36–38, 138

M

MacDonald, M., 26, 43, 44
Machado, P. P., 130
Malone, P., 24, 92, 111
McCormick, N. B., 24
McCubbin, H. I., 85
Mead, D. E., 26, 42
Moos, B. S., 26, 40, 41
Moos, R. H., 26, 40, 41
Mosher, D. L., 24
Murstein, B. I., 26, 43, 44

N

Neufeldt, S. A., 130

O

Obler, M., 24
O'Connor, D., 24
O'Gorman, E. C., 24
O'Grady, K. E., 24
Olson, D. H., 26, 39, 41, 85
Orlinsky, D. E., 130

P

Parks, B. K., 130
Patterson, D. G., 24
Patterson, J. M., 85
Pickard, C., 138
Piercy, F. P., 24, 92

Pinsof, W. M., 25, 78, 135
Portner, J., 26, 39, 41

R

Razin, A. M., 135
Reynolds, W. M., 16
Roberts, S. L., 26, 42
Rogers, L. E., 15, 27, 45, 81
Rust, J., 138

S

Scheier, I. H., 99, 112
Schiavi, R. C., 24
Schumm, W. R., 38
Sharpe, L., 24
Slosnerick, M., 24
Sollie, D. L., 24
Spanier, G., 26, 37
Spielberger, C. D., 79
Straus, M. A., 26, 44, 83

Stuart, F., 41
Stuart, R. B., 41, 42
Summers, K. J., 27, 45

V

Vatcher, G. M., 26, 42

W

Wallace, K. M., 26, 36–38,
    138
Watzlawick, P., 11, 14
Weis, D. L., 24
Weiss, R. L., 27, 43, 45
Williamson, D., 24, 92, 111
Wyne, B. A., 26, 42

Y

Yourglich, A., 24

Subject Index

A

Accountability, 118–146
  employer responsibilities, 119–123
  follow-up questionnaire, 139–146
  managed care responsibilities,
    123–131
      clinical personnel and practice,
        128–131
      contracts, benefits, and services,
        123–125
      ethical and legal considerations,
        126–128
      institutions and facilities, 126
  outcomes, 134–139
  overview of, 118
  therapist responsibilities, 132–134
Affect, initial interview, 3
Areas of Change Questionnaire, 42–43
Assessment
  crisis situations, 72–83
  of developmental transitions, 84–92.
    See also Developmental transitions
    assessment

individual–marital/family assessment,
  11–21. *See also* Individual–marital/
  family assessment
initial interview, 1–10. *See also* Initial
  interview
instrument selection for, 22–50. *See
  also* Instrument selection
managed care and, viii
systems approach, 93–117
  intergenerational family, 107–117
  nuclear family, 96–107
  overview of, 93–96
Assessment interview, case example,
  51–71
Attitudes, initial interview, 3

B

Beavers Interactional Scales, 27,
  45
Beck Depression Inventory, 16, 58,
  59, 60, 84, 85
Behavior, initial interview, 3
Beliefs, initial interview, 3

159

Benefits, accountability, managed
    care responsibilities, 123–125

C

Change sensitivity, instrument
    selection, individual–marital/
    family assessment, 13
Client history
  instrument selection, managed care
    and, 30–36
  presenting problem, initial interview,
    4–10
Client satisfaction, assessment,
    systems approach, 95
Cognition, initial interview, 3
Collateral contacts
  individual–marital/family assessment,
    11–12
  initial interview, presenting problem
    history, 10
  managed care and, vii–viii
Comprehensive Areas of Change
    Questionnaire, 26
Conflict Tactics Scale, 26, 44, 83
Contracts, accountability, managed
    care responsibilities, 123–125
Costs
    assessment, systems approach,
      95–96
    instrument selection, individual–
      marital/family assessment, 13–14
    managed care, employer responsi-
      bilities, 120–123
Crisis situations, case example, 72–83
Critical issues measures, instrument
    selection, 43–45

D

Daily Stress Inventory, 59, 60
Decision making, initial interview,
    1–10. *See also* Initial interview
Depression, individual–marital/
    family assessment, 15–17

Developmental transitions assess-
    ment, 84–92
  feedback using, 87–91
  findings, 87
  overview of, 84–87, 92
*Diagnostic and Statistical Manual of
    Mental Disorders (DSM-IV)*, V-
    Codes, managed care exclusion,
    vii, 132
Dyadic Adjustment Scale, 26, 37

E

Employer responsibilities, managed
    care, 119–123
Ethics
  accountability
    managed care responsibilities,
      126–128
    therapist responsibilities, 133
  managed care and, 10
Exchange Orientation Inventory, 26,
    43, 44
Expertise, instrument selection,
    individual–marital/family
    assessment, 13

F

FACES. *See* Family Adaptability and
    Cohesion Scale III: Couple
    Version
Facilities, accountability, managed
    care responsibilities, 126
Family Adaptability and Cohesion
    Scale III: Couple Version, 26,
    39, 40, 41
Family assessment. *See* Individual–
    marital/family assessment
Family Crisis Oriented Personal
    Evaluation Scales (F-COPES),
    85, 86, 87
Family Environment Scale, 26, 40–41
Family Inventory of Life Events and
    Changes, 85, 87

Family-of-Origin Scale, 24, 92
Follow-up questionnaire, accountability, 139–146
Functional Communication and Conflict Negotiation Adequacy Checklist, 27, 45

G

Golombok–Rust Inventory of Sexual Satisfaction, 138

I

Index of Sexual Satisfaction, 138
Individual–marital/family assessment, 11–21
  case example, 18–21
  conceptual issues, 14–21
    generally, 14–17
  instrument selection, 12–14. *See also* Instrument selection
  overview of, 11–12
  systems considerations, 17–18
Initial interview, 1–10
  overview of, 1–3
  presenting problem history, 4–10
Institutions, accountability, managed care responsibilities, 126
Instrument selection, 12–14, 22–50
  critical issues measures, 43–45
  marital diagnostic measures, 39–43
  marital dyad assessment, 25–27
  marital satisfaction measures, 36–39
  modified interview sequence procedure, 28–36
  pragmatic assessment, 45–50
  refinements, 22–25
Intergenerational family, assessment, systems approach, 107–117
Internalized Shame Scale, 24
Intervention, instrument selection for, 22–50. *See also* Instrument selection; Treatment
Interviews
  assessment interview, case example,

51–71
  initial interview, 1–10. *See also* Initial interview
Intimacy Needs Survey, 26, 39–40
IPAT Anxiety Scale Questionnaire, 99, 112, 116, 117

K

Kansas Marital Satisfaction Scale, 38

L

Law
  accountability, managed care responsibilities, 126–128
  managed care and, 10
Locke–Wallace Marital Adjustment Scale, 26, 36–38, 138

M

Managed care
  accountability in, 118–146. *See also* Accountability
  assessment and, viii
  client history, instrument selection, 30–36
  instrument selection, modified interview sequence procedure, 28–36
  V-Code exclusion, vii, 132
Marital diagnostic measures, instrument selection, 39–43
Marital dyad assessment, instrument selection, 25–27
Marital/family assessment. *See* Individual–marital/family assessment; Instrument selection
Marital Interaction Coding System, 27, 45
Marital Precounseling Inventory, 41–42
Marital satisfaction measures, instrument selection, 36–39
Mastery, initial interview, 3
Minnesota Multiphasic Personality Inventory (MMPI), 30
Mosher Guild Inventory, 24

N

Nuclear family, assessment, systems approach, 96–107

O

Outcomes
accountability, 134–139
assessment, systems approach, 94–95
initial interview, presenting problem history, 9

P

Patient history. *See* Client history
Personal Authority in the Family System Questionnaire, 24, 92, 111, 115, 117
Pragmatic Marital Assessment Questionnaire (PMAQ), 45–50, 61, 75–76, 85, 87, 110, 138
Praxis, instrument selection, individual–marital/family assessment, 13
Presenting problem
history, initial interview, 4–10
initial interview, 1–3
Pretreatment assessment, initial interview, 1–10. *See also* Initial interview
Problem codification, initial interview, 3
Psychiatric diagnoses, rationale for, 28–30

Q

Quality of Life Questionnaire, 85, 86–87

R

Referral, initial interview, presenting problem history, 4, 7

Relational Communication Coding System, 27, 45
Reliability, instrument selection, individual–marital/family assessment, 12
Resistance, initial interview, presenting problem history, 4

S

Services, accountability, managed care responsibilities, 123–125
Sex Anxiety Inventory, 24
Sex Education Liberalism Scale, 24
Sex Knowledge Inventory, 24
Sex-Love-Marriage Association Scale, 24
Sexual Anxiety Scale, 24
Sexual Attitudes and Beliefs Inventory, 24
Sexual Irrationality Questionnaire, 24
Sexual Orientation Method and Anxiety Questionnaire, 24
Sibling Systems Scale, 24
Situational analysis, initial interview, presenting problem history, 9–10
Spousal Inventory of Desired Changes and Relationship Barriers, 26, 42
State-Trait Anger Expression Inventory, 79
Suicide, individual–marital/family assessment, 16
Suicide Ideation Questionnaire, 16
Systems approach
assessment and, 93–117
intergenerational family, 107–117
nuclear family, 96–107
overview of, 93–96
individual–marital/family assessment, 15–17. *See also* Individual–marital/ family assessment

T

Theory–practice considerations. *See* Praxis

Therapist responsibilities, accountability, 132–134

Training, instrument selection, individual–marital/family assessment, 13

Treatment
goals of, initial interview, presenting problem history, 8–9
individual–marital/family assessment, 11–12
types of, viii

U

Universality, instrument selection, individual–marital/family assessment, 12

V

Validity, instrument selection, individual–marital/family assessment, 12

V-Code exclusion, managed care, vii, 132

Videotaping, critical issues measures, instrument selection, 44–45

Violence, critical issues measures, instrument selection, 44